Momentum, Direction, and Divergence

WILEY TRADER'S ADVANTAGE SERIES

Momentum, Direction, and Divergence

William Blau

Series Editor: Perry J. Kaufman

John Wiley & Sons, Inc.

New York • Chichester • Brisbane • Toronto • Singapore

Copyright © 1995 by William Blau
Published by John Wiley & Sons, Inc.

Library of Congress Cataloging-in-Publication Data:

Blau, William, 1926–
    Momentum, direction, and divergence / William Blau.
      p.   cm. — (Wiley trader's advantage series)
    Includes bibliographical references.
    ISBN 0-471-02729-4 (cloth)
    1. Stocks—Prices—Charts, diagrams, etc. I. Title. II. Series.
  HG4638.B55   1995
    332.63′22—dc20   94-38103
Printed in the United States of America
10 9 8 7 6 5 4 3

To Joan

ACKNOWLEDGMENTS

In 1982, I left my lifelong career as an electronics engineer. The choices were many and varied. I traveled. I did a lot of motorcycling, exploring the highways and back roads of America. I went back to school, where I studied art appreciation, music appreciation, gourmet cooking, and the art of investing. The latter adult education course was given at a local high school by a stockbroker.

The investment course caught my fancy—especially the part about commodities. I signed up with a commodities broker and started trading hogs on a daily basis. I had much to learn, but somehow I managed to make money and remain in black.

I soon realized there was a better way to trade. The personal computer was just beginning to make inroads in the investment community. Computer trading programs were becoming commercially available. My broker purchased one of the new PCs and a computer program called "CompuTrac." Shortly thereafter, I also purchased an IBM PC (with floppy disks—hard disks did not exist in those days) and became a CompuTrac subscriber. It was an educational experience and a real-world experience in trading using technical analysis as it existed at that time. I attended many of the TAG (Technical Analysis Group) Seminars sponsored by Tim Slater and his organization (now Telerate Seminars of Dow Jones Telerate, Inc.). I want to thank Tim and his staff for introducing me to the world of technical analysis. Today I am a product of those years of training and experience provided by TAG Seminars. Now I participate in the seminars as a guest speaker and also in seminars to private and institutional traders in many foreign financial centers.

I want to thank Thom Hartle and John Sweeney, editors of *Technical Analysis of Stocks and Commodities,* who encouraged me to write about the True Strength Index. Thanks also are due Jack Huston, publisher, for his permission to publish portions of magazine articles used in Chapters 2 and 3.

As a first-time book author, I wish to thank Perry Kaufman who provided editorial backup for the book. The manuscript editorial sessions were fruitful. The discussions dealing with both technical matters and methods of expression of ideas were memorable.

I wish also to express thanks to my many associates and friends of the Investment SIG (Special Interest Group) of the Boca Raton Computer Society, Inc., of Boca Raton, Florida, for their interest and encouragement. Special thanks go to Howard Leung and Peter Spinner for many spirited conversations on technical analysis and trading. I want to also thank Rich Ackerman for reviewing the manuscript for technical content and approach.

Technical trading can only be exploited if good tools are available. The tools of a good trader are experience, judgment, and a mathematical hierarchy provided by a good trading computer program. We are fortunate to have a program such as Omega TradeStation, which satisfies most of the needs of the stock and commodities trader. I wish to thank Bill Cruz and the staff of Omega Research, Inc., Miami, Florida, for giving me the opportunity, using TradeStation, to "do my own thing" as a trader.

WILLIAM BLAU

Boca Raton, Florida

THE TRADER'S ADVANTAGE SERIES PREFACE

The Trader's Advantage Series is a new concept in publishing for traders and analysts of futures, options, equity, and generally all world economic markets. Books in the series present single ideas with only that background information needed to understand the content. No long introductions, no definitions of the futures contract, clearing house, and order entry: Focused.

The futures and options industry is no longer in its infancy. From its role as an agricultural vehicle it has become the alterego of the most active world markets. The use of EFPs (exchange for physicals) in currency markets makes the selection of physical or futures markets transparent, in the same way the futures markets evolved into the official pricing vehicle for world grain. With a single telephone call, a trader or investment manager can hedge a stock portfolio, set a crossrate, perform a swap, or buy the protection of an inflation index. The classic regimes can no longer be clearly separated.

And this is just the beginning. Automated exchanges are penetrating traditional open outcry markets. Even now, from the time the transaction is completed in the pit, everything else is electronic. "Program trading" is the automated response to the analysis of a computerized ticker tape, and it is just the tip of the inevitable evolutionary process. Soon the executions will be computerized and then we won't be able to call anyone to complain about a fill. Perhaps we won't even have to place an order to get a fill.

Market literature has also evolved. Many of the books written on trading are introductory. Even those intended for more advanced audiences often include a review of contract specifications and market mechanics. There are very few books specifically targeted for the experienced and professional traders and analysts. *The Trader's Advantage Series* changes all that.

This series presents contributions by established professionals and exceptional research analysts. The authors' highly specialized talents have been applied primarily to futures, cash, and equity markets but are often generally applicable to price forecasting. Topics in the series will include trading systems and individual techniques, but all are a necessary part of the development process that is intrinsic to improving price forecasting and trading.

These works are creative, often state-of-the-art. They offer new techniques, in-depth analysis of current trading methods, or innovative and enlightening ways of looking at still unsolved problems. The ideas are explained in a clear, straightforward manner with frequent examples and illustrations. Because they do not contain unnecessary background material they are short and to the point. They require careful reading, study, and consideration. In exchange, they contribute knowledge to help build an unparalleled understanding of all areas of market analysis and forecasting.

Most traders seek leading indicators of price movement. In response, they are given combinations of price and volume, odd lots, and an assortment of indices to measure pieces and patterns of market movement. There have been entire books written on indicators. Each calculation is carefully designed to identify a particular type of price pattern and help make a better trading decision.

These indicators usually work in those situations for which they are intended, but that may not be very often. Other times they may look the same, but not apply. It is difficult to tell when to use the indicator, and when to ignore it. You often need one indicator to tell when to use another indicator. This all means that most efforts to create a robust indicator have failed. They are either an oversimplification of a complex problem, or they require so much interpretation that they make the total problem more complicated than it began.

· William Blau has focused on the two most important elements in technical analysis, *momentum* and *direction,* and added *divergence,* the most significant market inconsistency. The study and understanding of these elements is enough to assure successful trading.

Momentum is change. Mr. Blau shows that it is more productive to work with price change than directly with price. He then takes this and develops new indicators and techniques for trading, which show a remarkable amount of expertise. Among these are the True Strength Index, Ergodic Oscillator, and Stochastic Momentum Index. He ties this work into directional indicators and finally divergence.

Most of all, William Blau emphasizes the technique of *double smoothing.* He shows how the combination of price change and double smoothing provides a substitute for traditional trend following which has less lag. Less lag means more responsive trading and ultimately greater profits.

This book is filled with innovative, important trading techniques and many other new ideas. We are fortunate to have Mr. Blau share his work with us.

PERRY J. KAUFMAN

Wells River, Vermont

CONTENTS

1

INTRODUCTION

This book is about *price change*. It is about *double smoothing* as a means for making price change useful in trading stocks and futures. It is about new concepts for determining *when to* trade and, just as important, *when not to* trade.

Momentum is a name given to the technique of comparing prices at different times. For example, a price rise from one day to the next is an appropriate description of a one-day momentum. Indicators for assessing stocks and commodities are based on momentum when it is averaged (smoothed). A popular single-smoothed indicator is Wilder's *Relative Strength Index (RSI)*. Popular indicators that use double smoothing include Lane's *Slow Stochastic* and Appel's *Moving Average Convergence Divergence (MACD)*, (see References).

These techniques are presented for the benefit of traders who use computers to assist in their trading decisions. Readers who aspire to be traders can advance their knowledge of technical analysis of stocks and commodities. The subject matter revolves about indicators that are written as algebraic formulas. The use of the indicators involves timing of decisions to enter and exit the markets. To that extent, a knowledge of mathematics, notably algebra, is desirable.

Double-smoothed trading indicators are introduced in Chapters 2 through 7. Indicator formulas are presented along with examples taken from actual futures and stock price data. In many cases, the reader may reproduce the results of the examples as part of the learning process.

Trading is considered from the point of view of trend following. The ability to identify the trend and to obtain timely entries and exits is always important. Perhaps of greater significance is the ability to recognize the *lack* of trend during periods of flat prices or regions of congestion. It has been estimated that many markets are directionless more often than not. Under these conditions, it can be difficult to trade successfully. Slippage and commission charges become a large part of trading costs.

The problems of trading ranges, price congestion, and flat prices are addressed starting in Chapter 7 using a double-smoothed momentum indicator based on the high and low of the price bar. The indicator is shown to have properties that can be exploited to filter out (reject) trading ranges, congestion, and flat prices. There is no Holy Grail. There are many "ifs," "ands," and "buts" to be concerned about. However, the techniques introduced in Chapter 7 move us in the right direction.

Chapter 8 continues to address the problem of price congestion in trading for trend followers. Here the examples are based on the close-to-close double-smoothed *True Strength Index (TSI)* of Chapter 2.

The effects of price congestion on trading can also be reduced using other double-smoothed indicators. Chapter 9 demonstrates this using the *Stochastic Momentum Index (SMI)* first described in Chapter 3. A *Tick Volume Indicator (TVI)* is used in Chapter 10 to filter out trendless prices. The technique is useful for the day trader since it is unaffected by opening gaps.

In Chapter 11, Wilder's nonlinear processing in his ADX concept is adapted to any of the double-smoothed indicators in the book. An example using the True Strength Index is presented.

Chapter 12 deals with a new and promising concept of *slope divergence*. The technique is simple in concept and very useful for identification of trading ranges, congestion regions, and flat prices.

A number of computer trading programs permit traders to use their own indicators and formulate their individual trading decisions. This book uses *Omega TradeStation™*. Appendix B presents TradeStation code used for the indicators and techniques in the book. The code is also compatible with *Omega SuperCharts™*.

2

TRUE STRENGTH
INDEX

Our interest in technical analysis is due to our interest in making money. Charts are a historical expression of the marketplace. If we can buy a stock or commodity at a low price and sell it later at a higher price, we will have made money. Easily said—but not so easily done. It is a simple matter to view a chart and, in retrospect, see trends. Although the trend is embedded in noisy variations and may whipsaw about, the brain has that wonderful faculty for smoothing out the fluctuations and casting aside the noise. This is great on historical data but not too useful for prices we have not yet seen. There are traders who can define trends by looking at price charts as they unfold; however, the great majority of people require additional assistance.

Enter the computer. The computer, or more correctly, the computer trading program can average out the noise and present us with smooth curves so that trends, up or down, may be more readily identified. This is generally accomplished using a *moving average* of price usually based on the *close* of each bar interval. If the chart is very noisy, more averaging is required to smooth it out so that the trend, if present, may be seen. However, since the averaging process takes time to perform, the existence of the trend will also take time to unfold. A rally, for example, could be well in process before it is indicated by the moving average. It is a fact that moving averages performed on prices produce *lag*. The longer the moving average, the greater the lag although the benefit is smoother response.

It seems the computer has helped us with the chore of determining the presence of a trend in a noisy environment, but at a cost—lag. We all have experienced the lag of very smooth moving averages by entering a trend late and losing the initial portion of the trend; we also have experienced giving back a portion of the profits by exiting a trend late.

TRUE STRENGTH INDEX: *TSI* FORMULA

Figure 2–1 shows a bar graph of the S&P 500 Index, the celebrated "crash" of October 1987 with its True Strength Index plot below it. The True Strength Index (*TSI*) is a double-smoothed momentum indicator to be described shortly. Study the graphs closely. The *TSI* tracks the bar graph with little or no observable lag at major and intermediate turning points. The *TSI* graph is relatively smooth. An *exponential moving average (EMA)* is taken of the *TSI* and shown as a dotted *Signal Line*. When the *TSI* is above its Signal Line, the trend is up. A downtrend is indicated when the *TSI* is below its Signal Line.

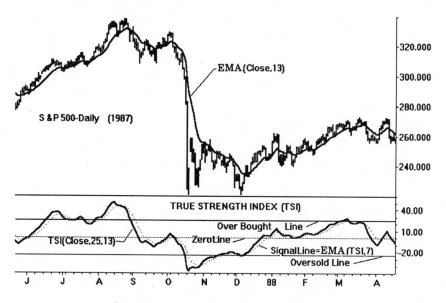

Figure 2–1   Basic Configuration of the *TSI*

Although prices can theoretically range from zero to unlimited levels, the *TSI* can range only from −100 to +100. Historically, prices related to a *TSI* scale tend to come to extreme values and reverse above (or below) set thresholds. In the example of Figure 2–1, prices are said to be historically *overbought,* high prices that are ready for reversal or pause, above a *TSI* threshold set at +25. Similarly, prices are said to be *oversold,* low prices, at a *TSI* threshold set at −25. This characteristic of defining high or low price categories is useful for trading purposes.

The *TSI* formula is given in Figure 2–2. It deals with a quantity called *momentum,* which is further explained in Figures 2–3 and 2–4. The numerator of the *TSI* formula represents *double smoothing of momentum.* This means we take an exponential moving average (*EMA*) of momentum for *r*-days and obtain a result. We now take an *EMA* of this result for *s*-days. We have thus made two sequential exponential

$$TSI(close,r,s) \ = \ 100^* \frac{EMA(EMA(mtm,r),s)}{EMA(EMA(|mtm|,r),s)}$$

In Numerator:

mtm	**= close[today] - close[yesterday]**
	(one-day momentum of the close)
EMA(mtm,r)	**= r-day EMA of mtm**
EMA(EMA(mtm,r),s)	**= s-day EMA of EMA(mtm,r)**
	(double-smoothing of mtm)

In Denominator:

|mtm|	**= absolute value of mtm**
EMA(|mtm|,r)	**= r-day EMA of absolute value of momentum**
EMA(EMA(|mtm|,r),s)	**= s-day EMA of EMA(|mtm|,r)**
	(double-smoothing of absolute value of momentum)

...The True Strength Index, TSI, is a "true" momentum indicator...

Figure 2–2 *TSI* Formula

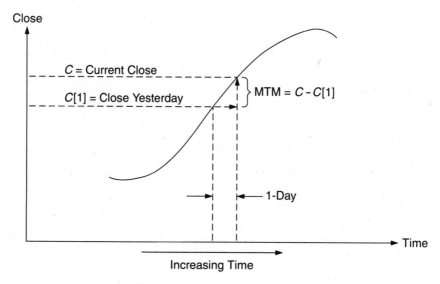

Figure 2–3 Momentum Defined

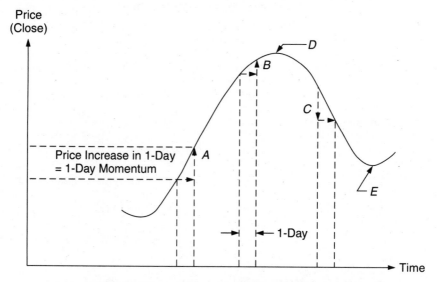

Figure 2–4 Price Momentum Basics

moving averages. As we shall see later on, this simple procedure performed on momentum can give *low lag, smooth curves* which also show trending characteristics of prices. The denominator of the *TSI* is the absolute value (a value that can only be positive . . . no negative signs) of momentum and is double-smoothed. The purpose of the denominator is to compress the range of the momentum to +100 and −100. Double smoothing is indicated on charts by the 2-place notation, *TSI*(close,25,13), of Figure 2–1, which means the *TSI* is based on the close with a first smoothing of 25 bars and a second smoothing of 13 bars. Please note that the order of smoothing does not change the end values of the *TSI* formula.

It is not necessary to be a mathematician to use the *TSI*. Once the formula is set in your computer, the *TSI* can be used as simply as you use moving averages. The numerator of the *TSI, double-smoothed momentum,* may be calculated on most computers that permit the user to take moving averages.

MOMENTUM DEFINED: PROPERTIES

Figure 2–3 shows a portion of an idealized (smooth) price curve. Consider it to be a curve of the closes of the price bars drawn as a continuous curve. The curve is rising. It has an upward, or positive, *slope.* Momentum is defined so as to measure the slope of the price curve on a day-to-day basis. If today's close is C, and yesterday's close is $C[1]$, then the 1-day momentum is defined as $mtm = C - C[1]$. In words, momentum equals today's close minus yesterday's close, the change in price over one day. With a rising curve, the momentum is a positive number shown graphically with an up-arrow.

Figure 2–4 depicts a number of different momentum situations. The curve shown has peaks and valleys with rising and falling sections. At point A, the price curve is rising and has positive momentum. At point B, the curve continues its upward ascent but at a slower pace. As a result, the 1-day momentum is smaller and is represented by the shorter upward arrow. Point D is the peak of the price curve, which is neither rising nor falling; at this point the curve has zero slope, or zero momentum. At point C, the price curve is going down; it has negative slope, negative momentum. The length of the downward arrow suggests the pace of the decline. Point E is a trough in the price curve. It has zero slope, zero momentum. *Momentum has desirable properties for investing and trading: It expresses the direction of the market, shows the amount of movement or pace of the market, and highlights turning points.*

ONE-DAY MOMENTUM

Figure 2–5 is a bar graph of AMGEN on a long bull market. Below it is plotted the 1-day momentum, close today minus close yesterday, from November through May. In contrast to Figures 2–3 and 2–4, it is noiselike in appearance. This is the real world of noisy variations. The closes are not a smooth upward curve. The trend is up but successive closes are not straight up. Examination reveals that the successive closes are sometimes higher and sometimes lower; the momentum shifts rapidly from up to down and vice versa appearing on the chart as up and down zero-crossings. The net effect is that a rally has been in progress. If anything, however, it appears that going to a momentum description has made things worse—less recognizable— more noisy—more difficult to identify the trend.

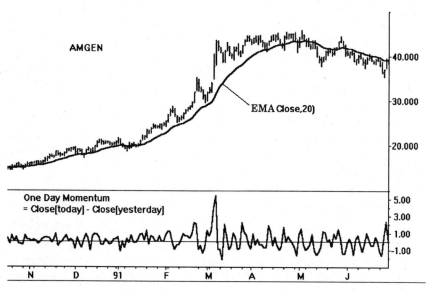

Figure 2–5   One-Day Momentum

MOMENTUM SMOOTHING

In Figure 2–6, a moving average is applied to the 1-day momentum of Figure 2–5. The effect is pronounced. The response is shifted away from the zero line, above zero. The upward bias of the trend is immediately recognizable. Intermediate swings in prices on the uptrend may also be identified. Rapidly fluctuating noise variations are also preserved but appear on the "envelope," the slower varying shifted response, which represents the trend. The moving average has a beneficial effect—it has screened the slowly varying component that represents the trend; the moving average has performed a correlation process to ascertain the presence of the trend.

    The desired result of applying a moving average to momentum data causes the trend line to vary slowly. The undesirable noise is still rapidly fluctuating. We wish to remove this noise without affecting the trend data. This is accomplished using a second moving average of short length as shown in Figure 2–7. Because of the short moving average, very little additional lag is introduced into the process. A comparison of Figures 2–6 and 2–7 shows that the trend and intermediate structure of the data are preserved and the noise is removed.

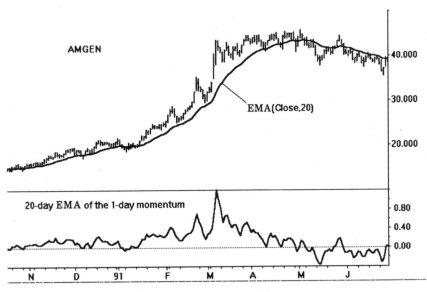

Figure 2–6 Single Smoothing of Momentum

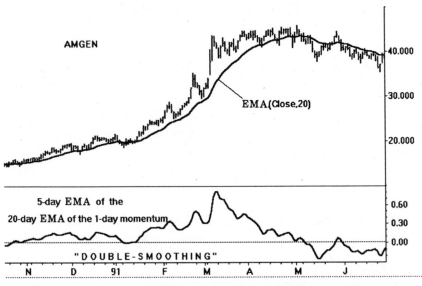

Figure 2–7 Double Smoothing of Momentum

MOVING AVERAGES

It is evident that moving averages play a key role in the development of indicators. What is a moving average? What is it that a moving average is actually performing? What are the effects of moving averages on prices when compared with moving averages on momentum?

Figure 2–8 shows a simplified explanation of the effect. The data on which a moving average is to be performed is a rectangular blip lasting 5 days, the top line of Figure 2–8. The moving average will have a length of 5 days as shown by the dotted moving window which is shifted in time over a 10-day interval. The rectangular window is shifted in time (to the right) so that its leading edge lines up with day 1. The shaded area on day 1 represents the overlap of the window with the data. The moving window is now incremented to day 2 (its leading edge lines up with day 2), and the overlap with the data is now observed to be twice as large. On the third day, the moving window is shifted in time by 3 days and the shaded overlap area with the data is three times as large as the first day. (The linear progression is unique to this example since we are dealing with rectangular data and a rectangular moving window of the same time duration.) The shaded overlap with the data represents the average performed by the moving window. For

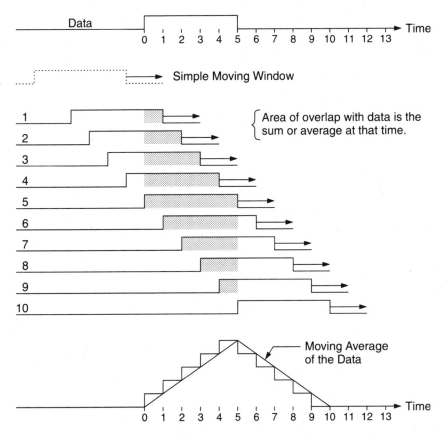

Figure 2–8 Anatomy of a Moving Average

each increment of time, there is a look-back of up to 5 days for making an average of all the data. The maximum look-back in our example occurs at day 5, at which time there is a complete overlap of the data, the largest average (largest shaded area). Progressing to day 6, the overlap area now diminishes. It further diminishes until at day 10 there is no longer any overlap with the data. The total day-by-day effect is summarized at the bottom of Figure 2–8 as an ascending staircase reaching its maximum value when the moving window completely overlaps the data. Thereafter with increasing time, the output of the moving average processing is a descending staircase.

What have we done with the moving average? The process of moving past one another in time and progressively averaging the overlap is the process of *correlation,* or convolution. We say that the data *correlates well* with the moving window when the data and moving window have similar appearance. When the shapes of the data and the moving window are identical (as in this example), we express this fact as *perfect correlation.* As the correlation increases, the moving average process (convolution) produces a larger more well-defined output, in this example, a definitive triangle.

Without going into great detail, consider what would happen if the data consisted of a train of short rectangles with successive rectangles going positive and negative. This is then to be correlated with a long positive rectangle as in our preceding example. In the moving average process, there will be days in which there is summing or averaging of positive and negative components, cancellations, so that a large well-defined output is not obtained. There is a lack of correlation of the data with the locally applied moving window, the moving average. Where correlation is lacking, the moving average rejects the rapidly fluctuating plus/minus train of rectangles—it "smoothes them out." The process of rejecting data not well correlated to the shape of the moving window is the process of smoothing the data. This is exactly what we do when we use a moving average on price data. The desired data more closely conform to our moving window than the noise fluctuations, which are removed by the moving average, or smoothing, process.

ANATOMY OF A RALLY: PRICE AND MOMENTUM

Our interest is in prices going up (or down) since it is in the *change* in prices that we make money. Figure 2–9 shows an idealized rally in prices and how it appears when subjected to the moving average process. The top line in the chart depicts prices at a constant level followed by a ramp, a rally at *A,* succeeded by prices at a constant level, *B.* In this simplified example, the moving window is a rectangle of time duration equal to the span of the rally, *A.* The result of performing the moving average is a rise with the rally but spread out over a time duration in excess of the time of the rally. The moving average reaches the end of the rise well after its actual completion: The moving average of the price rally is accompanied by *lag.*

In the lower panel of Figure 2–9, we examine the price rally when it is expressed in its momentum equivalent. Recalling that the one-bar momentum equals the price today minus the price yesterday, the momentum corresponding to the price rally at *A* is a rectangle. This

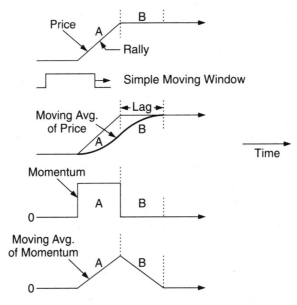

Figure 2-9 Anatomy of a Rally: Price and Momentum

is evident when we consider that successive prices during the rally at *A* are offset by the same amount giving rise to the flat momentum response during the rally. At the completion of the rally, the price plateau produces zero momentum since successive prices in this region have zero offset relative to each other.

A moving average (a moving rectangular window) is performed on the rectangular momentum, *A*. The result is immediately obtained as a triangular output (same as Figure 2–8). The triangle consists of a ramp, *A*, which rises in concert with the price rally. With the completion of the rally, a down ramp begins, *B*. The peak of the triangle marks the end of the rally. This *idealized* example shows zero lag suggesting that moving averages on momentum have a place in the description of prices.

SMOOTHED MOMENTUM AS A PROXY FOR PRICE

Moving averages performed on prices introduce lag. The longer the duration of the moving average, the greater is the lag. A 300-day moving average, for example, produces a tremendous amount of lag. *A single moving average performed on the momentum of price behaves in an altogether different manner. By contrast, the longer the duration of the moving average on momentum, the lower is the lag.* A 300-day moving average, for example, approximates a zero-lag situation. With emphasis, again: *A large moving average on momentum produces low lag price determination.*

Figure 2–10 displays this basic property of moving averages on momentum. The top panel is a plot of closing prices of the Deutsche mark. The middle panel refers to the numerator of the *TSI* termed the *Divergence Indicator (DI)* shown for single smoothing, (see also Figure 2–2). A large interval *300-day moving average of momentum* is seen to produce a curve that is a good approximation of price *shape*. The shape is also preserved for the compressed momentum, which defines the single-smoothed True Strength Index *(TSI)*. If the vertical scales at the right side of the chart were absent, we would have difficulty in determining which was which: *A large moving average of momentum provides an excellent stand-in for price—with the absence of lag.* This is demonstrated in the enlarged view of Figure 2–11.

We can reason from a mathematics point of view that large moving averages of momentum (the first derivative of price, the close) have, in the limit, the exact *shape* of price. We would expect this because the

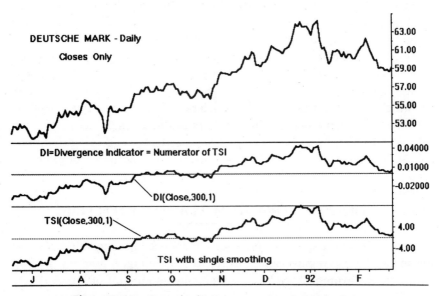

Figure 2–10   Smoothed Momentum as a Proxy for Price

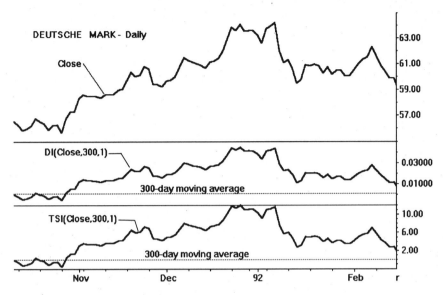

Figure 2-11   Smoothed Momentum as a Proxy for Price: Enlarged View

largest possible moving average encompasses all of the available data. In this extreme situation, the moving average (or the moving sum) becomes a cumulative sum of the momentum—it is the mathematical integration of the first derivative, which is identical (except for a constant of integration) to the original curve, the price or close. Theoretically, there is an absence of lag with this very long moving average of momentum. In addition, the type of moving average is secondary, whether it is an exponential, weighted, or a perfectly uniform simple moving average. The proof of the foregoing is similar to the proof of the fundamental theorem of integral calculus found in first-year college calculus textbooks.

DOUBLE SMOOTHING OF MOMENTUM

Since the *shape* of momentum and price are approximately equal for a very large moving average on momentum, we may perform functions, or operations, on either price or large moving average of momentum with the same results, with the exception of a scale factor. This is shown in Figure 2-12 for a 5-day moving average performed on the close (top panel) and a True Strength Index with sequential smoothings of 300

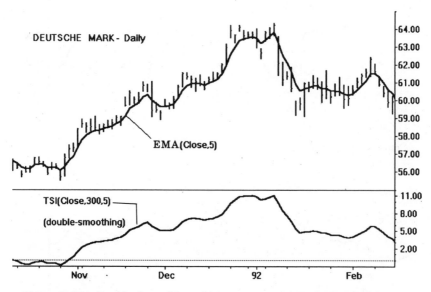

Figure 2–12 Double Smoothing of Momentum: Very Long Moving Average

days and 5 days, respectively. This then is the first blush of *double smoothing:* a noise-reduced, low-lag curve. The lag is that associated with the 5-day moving average. The shape of the *TSI*(close,300,5) approximates that of the 5-day *EMA* taken on the closes. *We can think of double smoothing of momentum as an excellent proxy for price when one of the moving averages is very large.*

We may further reduce the duration of the moving average from a very large 300-day value to 20 days while maintaining the short duration moving average of 5 days as displayed in Figure 2–13. At this point, we have a somewhat lower lag situation indicated by earlier turning points *P*. The effect produces divergences with prices at *A* and *B* where they did not exist before. Divergences are seen to be a function of smoothing times. How is a divergence interpreted? It is a comparison of prices (closes) with momentum (or momentum indicator) of prices. Consider the *down divergence* at *B*. A peak in the *TSI* marks the beginning of the divergence. This peak has a corresponding close. A second lower peak in the *TSI* marks the end of the divergence, *B*. The corresponding close is flat or higher than its preceding close at the start of the process. There is a divergence from the direction of the momentum indicator, which is in a down direction. This down divergence of the *TSI* from its price often signals an imminent price change, flat or down. Divergences

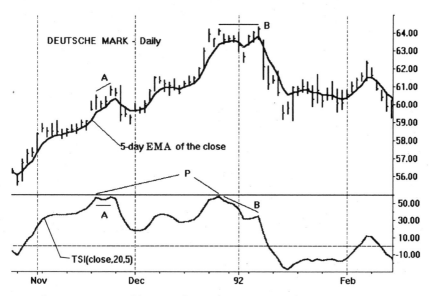

Figure 2–13   Double Smoothing of Momentum: Short Moving Average

can give powerful signals. Care must be exercised in their use and interpretation since false indications occur often. These can be lessened by confining them to overbought or oversold regions of the momentum indicator. A major drawback of the price divergence is that it is not defined while it is being formed.

A further iteration now is to have both moving averages "large," or comparable. Typically, we are talking of spans such as 13,13, or 20,40, or 100,20. Our interest embraces more than just noise-cleaning. Our interest is in *trending with respect to momentum* as opposed to trending with respect to price. One of the advantages for the trader is that turning points in momentum often precede those in price. Another is the appearance of divergences, which often signal imminent price changes as shown in Figure 2–13. With the *TSI*, the user can assign number positions representing how "overbought" or "oversold" prices are, based on prior history.

We are accustomed to expect lag in dealing with moving averages directly on prices. Double smoothing of prices will experience a lag for each level of smoothing. *Double smoothing of momentum of prices is a different phenomenon altogether.* Only one of the smoothings will produce lag. The longer duration moving average is operative in reproducing an approximation to the shape of price, without lag. The shorter duration moving average is responsible for lag. These properties are useful in controlling the shape of trending momentum curves that are not available on price curves.

TRADING WITH THE TRUE STRENGTH INDEX

The previous sections have described the properties and characteristics of double-smoothed momentum indicators using the True Strength Index as our test vehicle. It has been shown that double smoothing of momentum provides smooth and timely (low lag) price turning points and often can be used as a smoothed proxy for price. With these characteristics in mind, let us consider the *TSI* as it could appear as part of a trading system.

Our base system will be that of trend following. If we can determine when prices are trending, rising or falling, we then need a method of timing our entry to and exit from different levels of the trend. If the trend is rising, we wish to enter in the direction of rising prices—we wish to buy, and ideally when the trend direction changes, or ends—we wish to sell.

How do we define a trend? The first and obvious candidate for a measure of a trend is a moving average on prices. How do we determine our entry and/or exit points using the trend?

The Ergodic Oscillator

For entry and/or exit, we may use a fast oscillator such as the Slow Stochastic. This indicator is one of the most popular today and much data and information about it is available in the open literature (see e.g., article by originator, George Lane, listed in References).

Since our exposition is about the True Strength Index, we shall employ a similar oscillator based on the True Strength Index called the *Ergodic oscillator,* or simply, the *Ergodic.* The oscillator consists of two parts: the Ergodic and its Signal Line given by

$$Ergodic(\text{Close},r) = TSI(\text{Close},r,5)$$

$$SignalLine(\text{Close},r) = EMA(TSI(\text{Close},r,5),5).$$

The Ergodic is the double-smoothed *TSI* with one *EMA* smoothing fixed at five price bars. A further *EMA* smoothing by a fixed amount of five price bars produces its Signal Line. The Ergodic (with its Signal Line) is shown in the middle panel of Figure 2–14 for the daily Deutsche mark. For comparison, the Stochastic oscillator is displayed in the bottom panel.

Both oscillators have the same smoothing of $r = 20$ days. In mid-February, each oscillator crosses its respective signal line in a timely fashion indicating a down move in concert with the downturn of the moving average on the price chart. The oversold and overbought lines for the Stochastic are at 20 and 80. The oversold and overbought lines for the Ergodic are at -20 and $+20$. Both oscillators reach their thresholds at the same time. The Stochastic quickly "bottoms out" at an extreme oversold condition as the price decline continues into March. In March, the Stochastic and its Signal Line are compressed together with crossovers.

The Ergodic is more forgiving in its oversold region. In March, it also goes far into its oversold region, down below -80. Since its oversold threshold is at -20, there is ample room to move *without compression*. As a result, the Ergodic correctly registers the long decline in prices. Because the Stochastic rapidly traverses the distance between its compressed overbought and oversold regions, it is somewhat faster than the

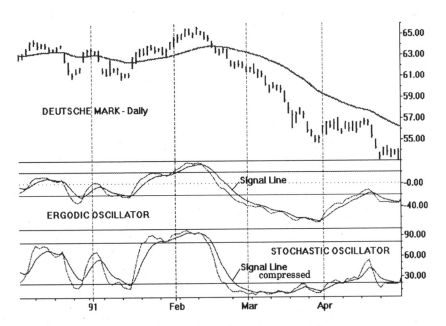

Figure 2–14 Ergodic and Stochastic Oscillators

Ergodic for the same number of days of smoothing. However, it does have the compression problem with long rallies and declines, which is not so prevalent with the Ergodic. Otherwise most problems and cautions in the use of the Stochastic also apply to the Ergodic oscillator.

Trading Ergodics with the Trend

We now have in place the basic elements of a trading system. The trend is defined by a moving average on price. The fast *TSI*, the ergodic oscillator, can provide the entry and/or exit points. We take a position when the slope of the trend, the moving average on price, and the slope of the Ergodic oscillator are in the same direction. We exit or stand aside when slopes are of opposite directions. A basic system demonstrating this principle is depicted in Figure 2–15 for the daily Deutsche mark.

Possible rules for trading could be as follows:

System 1

1. Enter or hold a position only when the slope of the Ergodic Signal Line has the same direction as the trend.

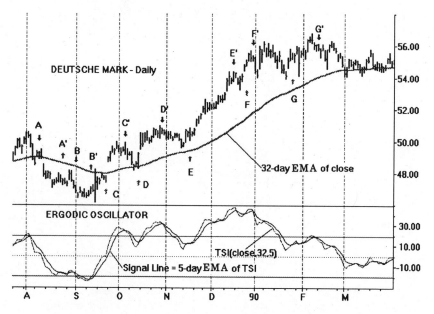

Figure 2–15 Trading with the Ergodic Oscillator

2. Stand aside when the slope of the Ergodic Signal Line is in the opposite direction of the trend.

3. Enter or exit a position when the Ergodic and its Signal Line cross.

A variation of System 1 is:

System 2

1. Same as System 1.

2. Same as System 1.

3. Enter a position when the Ergodic and its Signal Line cross in the direction of the trend. See also (1).

4. Exit a position when the Ergodic reverses its direction.

A third variation of System 1 is:

System 3

1. Enter or hold a position only when the slope of the Ergodic Signal Line is in the same direction as the trend.

2. Exit a position or stand aside when the slope of the Ergodic Signal Line is in the opposite direction as the trend.

Other variations are possible. The following description of System 1 will demonstrate the general technique.

Referring to Figure 2–15, the *EMA* of the close is for 32 days; the Ergodic oscillator has a 32-day *EMA*. In early August, the Signal Line is first to slope downward followed by the 32-day moving average, the trend. We enter with a sell order at point *A*. Prices recede, and then at point *A'*, the ergodic makes an upward crossover of its Signal Line and we exit the trade with a buy order. A downward crossover occurs shortly thereafter in early September. The trade if exercised would be a short position from *B* to *B'*. The trade may not be exercised since it occurs in oversold territory of the Ergodic.

The next trade starts at point *C* as the trend turns up. At this point, the Ergodic is already rising. The trade is completed at *C'* with a down crossover in the Ergodic oscillator. The next trade in the rally is a buy entry at *D* which is offset at a higher price at *D'*. The rally continues its upward journey commencing at point *E* going deeply into overbought territory—without compression. The exit is made at *E'*. An additional small jump up is made by the trade from *F* to *F'*. The last trade in the rally is made from *G* to *G'* just before the trend flattens out.

Trading Ergodics with a Slow TSI Trend

There are other candidates for the definition of the trend. Certainly the moving average on price qualified. What about a slow double-smoothed momentum indicator such as the True Strength Index? Refer to Figure 2–16, which shows a slow *TSI*(close,64,64) plotted against the daily Deutsche mark.

The main turning points in Figure 2–16 are evident with low lag despite the long moving averages of 64 days in each of the two smoothings. When the Deutsche mark trends, the slow *TSI* also trends. However, there is not always a one-to-one correspondence between price direction and *TSI* direction. This occurs in the first few months of 1990 when prices go into a trading range, a region of congestion. In

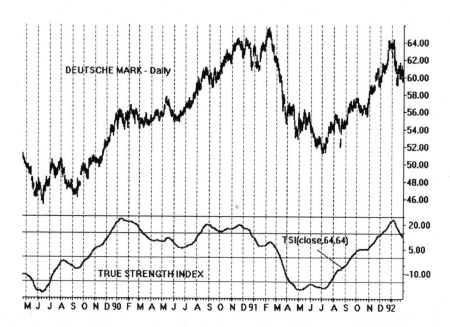

Figure 2–16 Slow *TSI* Trend

these regions, the *TSI* continues to slope while prices are flat. This suggests that the double-smoothed momentum indicator may be an excellent smooth and timely substitute for price while prices are trending. While prices are in congestion, the indicator may not be entirely satisfactory as a substitute in its current form.

Using the slow *TSI* to *define* the trend presents special characteristics not available when a moving average on price is used to define the trend. Long moving averages based on momentum do not appreciably increase the lag of turning points as do those based on price. Long moving averages are required in trend definition for smooth and slowly varying transitions. A slow *TSI* trend has the property of specifying overbought and oversold regions based on historical data. In Figure 2–16, for example, the daily Deutsche mark tended to be in overbought territory when it exceeded a threshold of +15. Similarly, oversold territory corresponded to a region of the slow *TSI* that was less than −15. When the slow *TSI* trend exceeds these thresholds, it warns the trader of a possible reversal of prices, or the end of a price rally or decline based on previous history.

Other characteristics of great importance for trading are discussed in Chapter 7, "Directional Trending," and Chapter 8, "True Strength Directional Trending." Here we examine the trading possibilities of trading Ergodics going with a slow *TSI* trend as shown in Figure 2–17. We have selected an example that includes both a trading range and a deep trend to show the effect. Three systems may be considered as before with the moving average trend. The rules presented there remain the same except the "trend" is now produced by the slow *TSI* trend.

The Deutsche mark chart shows a trading range from the beginning of November 1990 through January 1991. The slow *TSI* is in overbought territory so that caution should be exercised in taking a long position. We will always go with the trend using System 1 rules to demonstrate the effect of the trading range. The first entry is long at *A* which is offset at *A'* for a small gain. The second entry is short at *B* when the trend direction turns down, and the Ergodic is also down. This is quickly reversed on the Ergodic prompting an exit from the trade at *B'* for a small loss. The short trade from *C* to *C'* produces a small gain and the succeeding short trade from *D* to *D'* sustains a small loss. There are four trades with small gains and losses (excluding commission and slippage) due to the congestion regions in a 3-month interval. In mid-January, the (slow *TSI*) trend turns up, and we enter long at point *E*

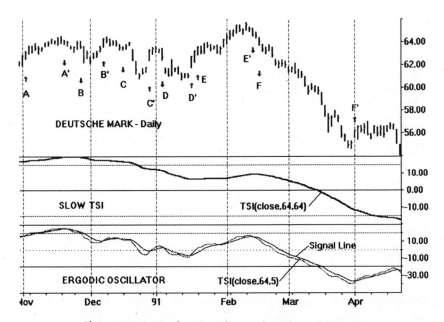

Figure 2–17 Trading Ergodics with a Slow *TSI* Trend

confirmed by the Ergodic, which had turned up earlier. The position is held until we are bumped out by a downturn in the Ergodic at point *E'*— a nice gain. At point *F* the trend turns down, and we enter short since the Ergodic is already down. We hold the position from mid-February until the beginning of April when the Ergodic ends the trade at *F'*.

Ideally we would like to eliminate the in-and-out trading that occurred in the congestion region because commission and slippage can add up.

3

STOCHASTIC
MOMENTUM

We begin this chapter by reviewing the very useful stochastic formulas attributed to and popularized by Dr. George Lane.

LANE'S STOCHASTICS

There are two formulas: the *Fast Stochastic* and the *Slow Stochastic.* The unsmoothed (fast) stochastic formula is given by

$$k = 100 \; \frac{\text{close} - LL(q)}{HH(q) - LL(q)}$$

where

$HH(q)$ = the highest high in the last q price bars

$LL(q)$ = the lowest low in the last q price bars.

A graph of the 1987 DJ Industrials with the *Fast Stochastic* appears in Figure 3–1. The Fast Stochastic shown in the middle panel can vary over a range of zero to 100. It often oscillates rapidly between overbought and oversold regions with respective thresholds set at 80 and 20.

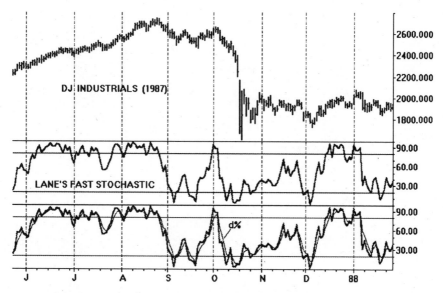

Figure 3–1 Lane's Fast Stochastic

The indicator is seen to be very timely with turning points that often lead price turning points. The price paid for this desirable timeliness is noise giving rise to many possible false indications. A large amount of the noise is removed by using a crossover system based on the Fast Stochastic and a Signal Line, $d\%$, which is the 3-day simple moving average (SMA) of the Fast Stochastic. A buy action is indicated when the Stochastic crosses above its Signal Line. A sell action is indicated when the Stochastic crosses below its Signal Line.

Use of the 3-day Signal Line aids greatly in the reduction of false indications. However, false indications still occur too often. This prompts the use of an additional 3-day SMA smoothing as shown in Figure 3–2. The first smoothing is called the Slow Stochastic, $d\%$, which has its associated 3-day SMA Signal Line called Slow $d\%$. Observation of Figure 3–2 shows the useful smoothness and timeliness that is responsible for the Slow Stochastic's great popularity with traders.

One of the popular forms of the slow stochastic is given by

$$d\% = 100 \; \frac{SMA(3) \text{ of } (close - LL(q))}{SMA(3) \text{ of } (HH(q) - LL(q))}$$

where $SMA(3)$ is the 3-day simple moving average.

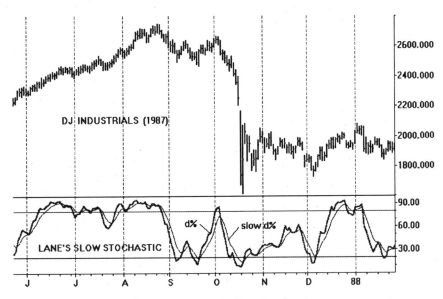

Figure 3-2 Lane's Slow Stochastic

DOUBLE-SMOOTHED STOCHASTICS

We have observed the marked improvement of the slow stochastic over the fast stochastic. We shall explore this effect using a general formulation called the *DS-Stochastic* given by

$$DS(q,r,s) = 100 \, \frac{EMA(EMA(\text{close} - LL(q),r),s)}{EMA(EMA(HH(q) - LL(q),r),s)}$$

where

close $- LL(q)$ = numerator of Lane's Fast Stochastic

$EMA(\text{close} - LL(q),r)$ = r-day exponential moving average
                           (EMA) of close $- LL(q)$

$EMA(EMA(\text{close} - LL(q),r),s) =$
  s-day EMA of $EMA(\text{close} - LL(q),r)$
  = double (EMA) smoothing of numerator

and similarly for the denominator.

Figure 3-3 depicts a train of high, low, close, price bars. The dark bar on the right side describes the range, $HH(q) - LL(q)$, assumed by

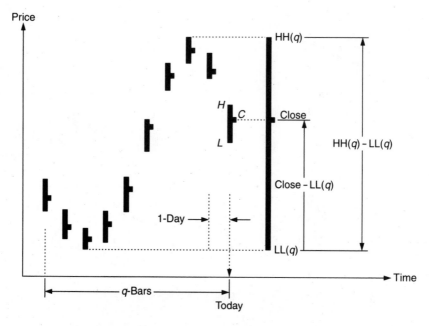

Figure 3–3   DS-Stochastics

the price bars in a look-back of q-bars. The raw stochastic formula, $DS(q,1,1)$, represents where the current close is relative to the low point of the stochastic range. A close near the upper portion of the range will be near the highest high in the most recent q-bars.

STOCHASTIC MOMENTUM

Figure 3–4 shows the same train of high, low, close price bars but with different notation. The stochastic range remains unchanged. The close, however, is now referenced to the midpoint $0.5 \times (HH(q) + LL(q))$ of the range.

The distance of the current close from the midpoint defines *stochastic momentum* as

$$SM(q) = \text{close} - 0.5 \times (HH(q) + LL(q)).$$

As a momentum, $SM(q)$ takes on positive and negative values. The magnitude of the momentum is determined by how large a displacement there is of the close relative to the midpoint of the range. When

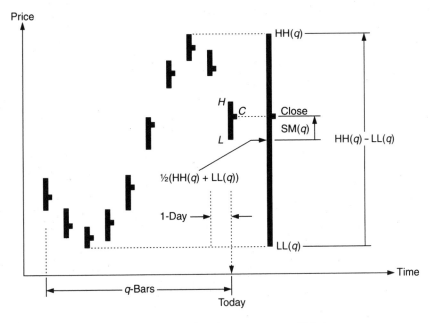

Figure 3–4 Stochastic Momentum, $SM(q)$

the close is greater than the midpoint of the range, the stochastic momentum is positive. The largest plus value occurs when the close equals $HH(q)$. The stochastic momentum takes on negative values when the close is less than the midpoint having its greatest negative value when it is equal to the lowest low of the past q-bars.

A comparison is made in Figure 3–5 between the close momentum and stochastic momentum. "Close momentum" is the close, 20 days ago, subtracted from today's close. With stochastic momentum, a *function* of the close 20 days ago is subtracted from today's close. The similarity between the two is evident in Figure 3–5.

STOCHASTIC MOMENTUM INDEX

Embracing stochastic momentum, the *Stochastic Momentum Index (SMI)* is now formulated as:

$$SMI(q,r,s) = 100 \frac{EMA(EMA(SM(q),r),s)}{0.5 \times EMA(EMA(HH(q) - LL(q),r),s)}$$

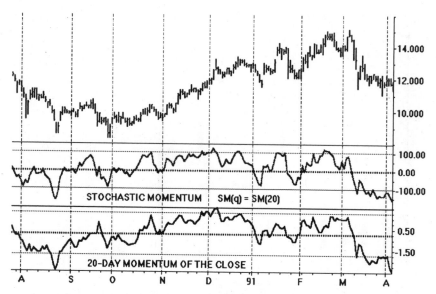

Figure 3–5 Close Momentum versus Stochastic Momentum

where *SM(q)* is *Stochastic Momentum* with a *q*-day look-back. The *SMI* is the bipolar (plus, minus) form of the *DS*-Stochastic which is always greater than zero. Both have the same shape.

The basic configuration of the Stochastic Momentum Index is shown in Figure 3–6 for a q = 13-day look-back with an *EMA* smoothing of 25 days. The indicator maps prices into a corresponding range from −100 to +100 on its scale. Prices are considered to be at "high" levels when the indicator is above its threshold overbought line (here set at +40). Prices are said to be at "low" levels when the indicator is below its threshold oversold line (here set at −40). The Signal Line shown is the *EMA* of *SMI(q,r,s)*. It is normally in the range of 3 to 12 bars. When the *SMI* is above its Signal Line, a price uptrend is indicated; a downtrend is defined when the *SMI* is below its Signal Line.

Double smoothing in the Stochastic Momentum Index SMI(q,r,s) is obtained by using any two of the q,r,s parameters while holding the remaining parameter fixed. Smoothing is readily evident in the *r,s* parameters because they represent direct exponential moving averages. Smoothing is also intrinsic to the *q* parameter describing Stochastic Momentum, *SM(q)*. See Figure 3–7 for the smoothing effect of the cumulative sum of the Stochastic Momentum. The result is comparable to taking an *EMA* of the close.

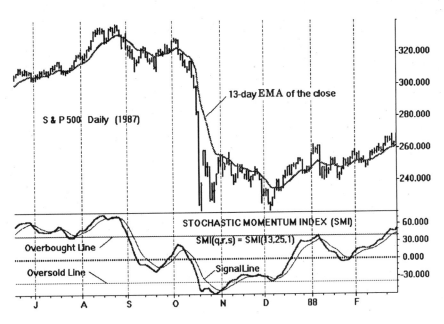

Figure 3-6 Stochastic Momentum Index: Basic Configuration

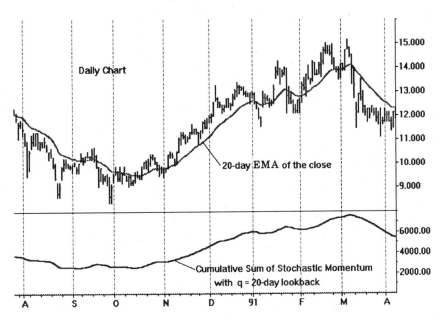

Figure 3-7 Smoothing Effect of Stochastic Momentum

STOCHASTIC MOMENTUM AS A PROXY FOR PRICE

When the Stochastic Momentum is taken over a very large interval (*SM(q)* where *q* is a very large number), the Stochastic Momentum takes on the characteristics of price *shape*. Figure 3–8 shows the stochastic momentum, *SM(300)* for *q* = 300, in the middle panel. This is the numerator of the Stochastic Momentum Index that is graphed in the bottom panel. It is observed that the shapes of panels are essentially the same. The *SMI* provides a +100 and −100 amplitude normalization. If the number scales on the right of the charts had been omitted, a user would be hard pressed to determine which was the close curve and which was the Stochastic Momentum.

Figure 3–9 shows the large-interval Stochastic Momentum (the first "smoothing" for *q* = 300-day) with a second (*EMA*) smoothing of 5 days. The result is a stripping away of the high frequency noise fluctuations producing a smoother curve. Because a short-duration *EMA* is employed, the introduction of lag (delay due to moving average effects) is minimal.

Figure 3–9 shows *double smoothing* using the parameter pair: *q,r*. The only lag introduced was due to the *r*-day *EMA*. The *q*-day

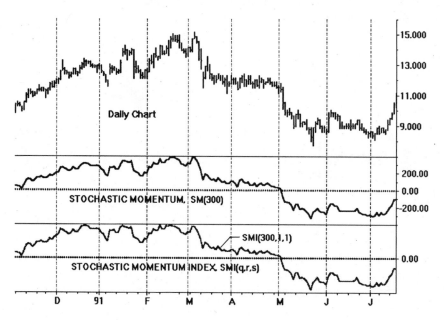

Figure 3-8 Stochastic Momentum as a Proxy for Price: Very Large Interval

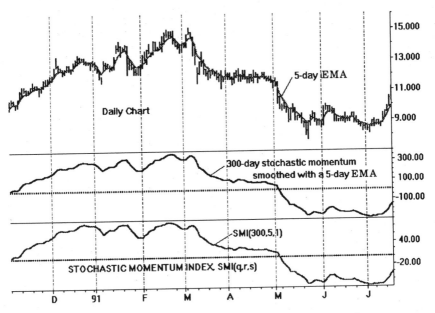

Figure 3–9 Stochastic Momentum Smoothing for Noise Reduction

Stochastic Momentum did not (ideally) produce any lag although $q = 300$ is a very large number of days. This is a very important characteristic of double-smoothed momentum indicators: Generally, *one of the smoothing functions will be of long duration; the other will be of shorter or equal duration. Only one will (ideally) introduce lag.* This is certainly not the case when moving averages are taken on price: A 300-day span for a moving average on price produces a great deal of lag. *This feature of double-smoothing of momentum indicators is fundamental to their timeliness and smoothness as indicators for stocks and commodities.* Two of the most popular indicators in current usage are the Slow Stochastic and the *MACD* (moving average convergence divergence), which both use double smoothing.

Normally, the very long time spans of 300 days are rarely used. Figure 3–10 shows a stochastic of $q = 20$-days with $r = 5$ days of *EMA* smoothing. (With $s = 1$, the pair: q,r provides double smoothing.) The Stochastic Momentum, after double smoothing, is seen (middle panel) to be timely and relatively free of noise variations. The $SMI(q,r,s) = SMI(20,5,1)$ is noted to be similar in appearance. Divergences appear when smaller time spans are used. A down divergence is identified with points A and B, or A and C, indicating a possible end to the price

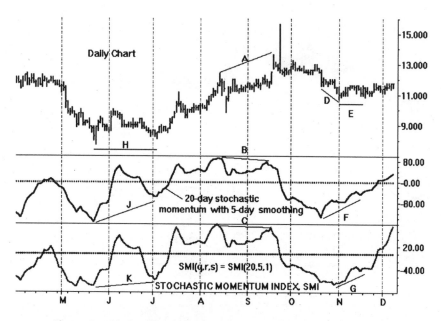

Figure 3–10 Stochastic Momentum Smoothing: Shorter Interval

rally. An up divergence is noted by points *H* and *J*, or *H* and *K*. Except for the regions *F* and *G*, the shapes of the middle and bottom panels are almost identical.

The Slow Stochastic and the Stochastic Momentum Index are compared in Figure 3–11. They approximate each other closely in terms of shape. The small disparity between the two shapes is due to the use of an exponential moving average (5-day) in the *SMI* versus a simple moving average (3-day) in the slow stochastic.

A departure from the Slow Stochastic is made in Figure 3–12 by increasing the *EMA* smoothing interval from 5 days to 20 days producing $SMI(q,r,s) = SMI(20,20,1)$. The Stochastic Momentum Index now appears to trend as prices trend. (The Slow Stochastic is included for the purpose of comparison). The major turning points are highlighted in a timely manner with lag less than, or equal to, that produced by the same moving average applied directly to price. Divergences now clearly appear at *B, C, D, E,* and *F.* A continuing divergence from the beginning of *B* to *C* signals the end of a price rally, or the beginning of a decline.

At *A*, the slope of the *SMI* trends up with prices. At *A*, the Slow Stochastic remains noisily flat in an overbought region. As shown,

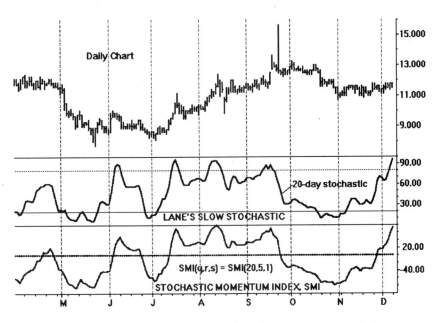

Figure 3–11 Slow Stochastic and Stochastic Momentum Index

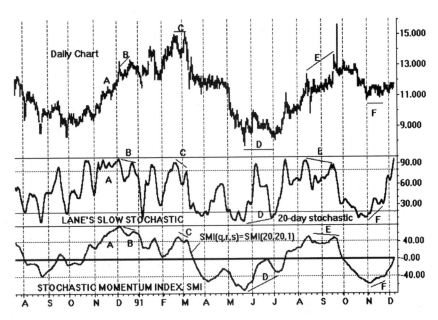

Figure 3–12 Increasing the *EMA* Smoothing Interval

the Stochastic Momentum Index is slowly varying showing price trends, major turning points and labeling of turning points by way of divergences with price.

The Slow Stochastic may now be used as an entry (or exit) vehicle for trading . . . with the Stochastic Momentum Index defining the trend in prices. An example of this approach can be seen in Figure 3–13 for $SMI(q,r,s) = SMI(20,60,1)$ defining the trend and a 20-day Slow Stochastic. Note the smoothness of the SMI, by increasing the EMA period to 60 days, with essentially very little additional lag introduction at the major turning points. Divergences on the SMI now exist only at D and G. The divergences that were at B, C, E and F are now absent. The major turning point in March is keyed by the long divergence G and is further supported by the Slow Stochastic divergence at C.

Long trends are often troublesome to those indicators that are inherently oscillators. Broadly speaking, when the duration of the trend exceeds the indicator's natural period of oscillation, the indicator may not properly show the direction of the trend. In the middle graph of Figure 3–14, $SMI(q,r,s) = SMI(20,20,1)$ is timely and smooth. However, it gives erroneous indications of the trend when the price trend is of very long duration. Starting in April, it indicates an uptrend while, in fact, prices continue to decline. The bottom panel of Figure 3–14,

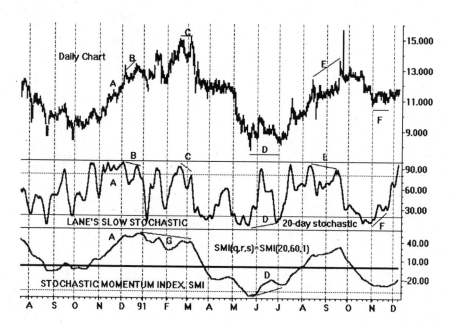

Figure 3–13 Further Increase of *EMA* Smoothing Interval

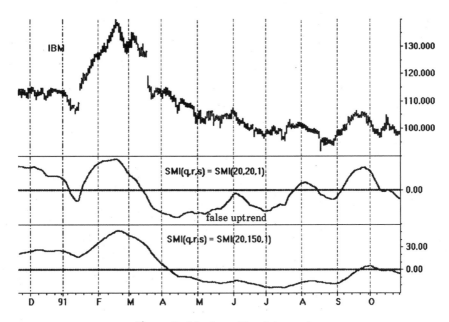

Figure 3–14 Long Trend Anomaly

SMI(20,150,1) removes the error so that the indicator again trends correctly with price. Timeliness and smoothness are present with very little additional lag. The lag is determined by the smallest value of *q* and *r* in the Stochastic Momentum Index, *SMI*(*q*,*r*,1). The turning points to be retained, the *major* turning points, are filtered by the largest value of the double smoothing *(q,r)* parameters. In Figure 3–14, the anomaly of having a downtrend in prices erroneously indicated is corrected by increasing the *r* parameter from 20 to 150.

TWO-DAY STOCHASTICS

When *q* = 2, there are two price bars in the look-back period as shown in Figure 3–15. The Stochastic Momentum for two price bars is

$$SM(2) = \text{close} - 0.5 \times (HH(2) + LL(2)).$$

To determine if the *2-day stochastic* is a reasonable proxy for price, a large (300-day) moving average is used in the Stochastic Momentum Index, *SMI*(*q*,*r*,*s*) = *SMI*(2,300,1). Comparison with the price chart on

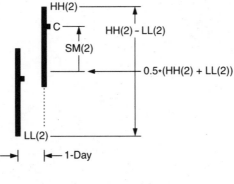

$$SM(2) = C - 0.5 \cdot (HH(2) + LL(2))$$

Figure 3–15 Two-Day Momentum

Figure 3–16 reveals it to be an excellent substitute for price. An example of 2-day stochastics is shown in Figure 3–17 for Treasury bonds where $SMI(q,r,s) = SMI(2,25,12)$. The fixed parameter is $q = 2$. The two-variable parameters for double smoothing are the r-day *EMA*, which is subsequently smoothed by an s-day *EMA*. The effect of the double smoothing is to remove high-frequency fluctuations obtaining

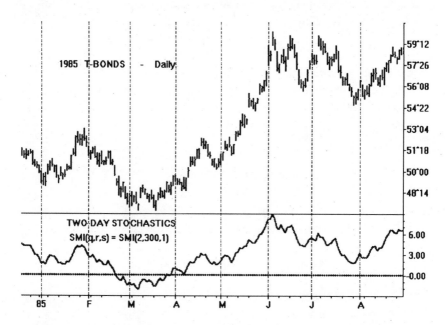

Figure 3–16 Two-Day Stochastics as a Proxy for Price

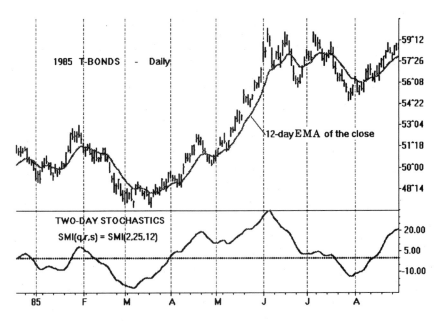

Figure 3–17 Two-Day Stochastics on T-Bonds

a relatively smooth trending curve. The curve is seen to be timely (low lag) with access to major turning points in prices. The timeliness is noteworthy when compared with a similar 12-day exponential moving average on the close.

An interesting situation is depicted in Figure 3–18: the effect of a key reversal pattern. A key reversal occurring in mid-September produces a 2-day Stochastic Momentum Index (*SMI*) that has a curve markedly different from a True Strength Index (*TSI*) curve both using the same smoothing parameters. The *TSI*(close,40,20) tracks the close-to-close price curve while remaining unaffected by the key reversal. However, the long spike of the key reversal has a dramatic response with the 2-day *SMI*(2,40,20). This is to be expected because 2-day stochastics are very sensitive to the location of the close relative to the extreme prices today and yesterday. Note the sudden drop in the response of the *SMI*(2,40,20) detecting the presence of the key reversal pattern.

The Two-Day Stochastic Oscillator

Lane's slow stochastic is an oscillator based on the past q-days. (See $d\%$ formula at beginning of chapter and Figures 3–1 and 3–2). Can we devise a stochastic oscillator based on the Stochastic Momentum Index

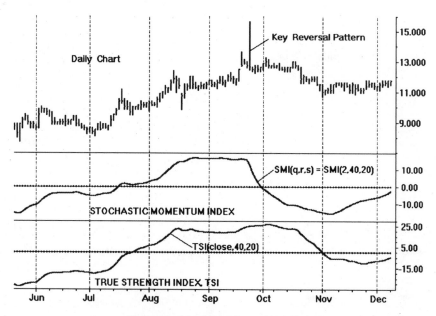

Figure 3–18 Key Reversal Pattern

with a q = 2-day look-back? The answer is yes. Is the response different from Lane's stochastic oscillator? Again, the answer is yes.

Let us define the 2-day stochastic oscillator and its associated signal line by:

$$2d\text{Stochastic}(r) = SMI(2,r,5)$$

$$2d\text{SignalLine}(r) = EMA(SMI(2,r,5),5)$$

The 2-day stochastic is defined for $SMI(q,r,s) = SMI(2,r,5)$ where a fixed look-back of 2 days is used and a fixed *EMA* smoothing of (nominally) s = 5 days is invoked. This again is *double smoothing*. The Signal Line is defined as the 5-day *EMA* of the 2-day stochastic. The use of a 5-day *EMA* is arbitrary depending on volatility of price conditions. The range of the *EMA* will generally fall between 3 and 12 days.

A plot of the 2-day stochastic with r = 32 and a 7-day *EMA* Signal Line is shown in Figure 3–19 for the daily Deutsche mark. Lane's 32-day Slow Stochastic and the Ergodic oscillator (based on the True Strength Index, *TSI*) with a 7-day *EMA* Signal Line are also shown for comparison. It is apparent that the 2-day stochastic oscillator and the

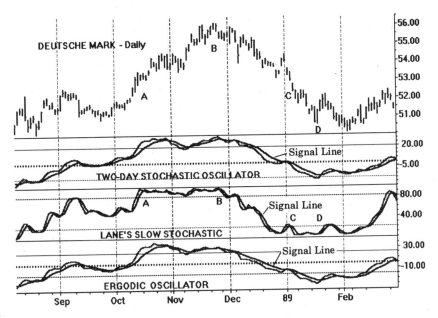

Figure 3–19 Two-Day Stochastic Oscillator

Ergodic oscillator are similar to each other: Both track prices smoothly and timely (low lag) as prices trend and change direction. The slow stochastic is somewhat more timely but registers compression effects. As prices trend up from points *A* to *B,* the slow stochastic is in its overbought region noisily intertwined with its signal line.

Prices decline from *B* to *C.* The 2-day stochastic and ergodic also decline going below their signal lines. The slow stochastic also declines but not smoothly: It oscillates above and below its signal line as it declines. Prices decline further between points *C* and *D* and are appropriately indicated by the 2-day stochastic and the Ergodic. The Slow Stochastic is now registering a flat response in its oversold region: Compression again. As shown in Figure 3–19, the Slow Stochastic would generate many false trades in a compression region such as *A* to *B.*

Trading with these oscillators can be as described in Chapter 2 for the Ergodic oscillator. The simplest policy, for example, could be to buy when the oscillator crosses above its signal line and to sell when the oscillator crosses below its signal line, subject to other trading system constraints. The Ergodic and 2-day stochastics do not exhibit compression effects to the extent of the Slow Stochastic and consequently generate fewer false trades.

ONE-DAY STOCHASTICS

The Stochastic Momentum Index for $q = 1$ is shown in Figure 3–20. When $q = 1$, the stochastic momentum is *defined* within the highest high and lowest low of the day:

$$SM(1) = \text{1-day stochastic momentum}$$

$$= \text{close} - 0.5 \times (\text{high} + \text{low}).$$

The Stochastic Momentum Index becomes:

$$SMI(1,r,s,) = 100 \ \frac{EMA(EMA(SM(1),r),s)}{0.5 \times EMA(EMA(\text{high-low},r,s))}$$

The *1-day stochastic* is sensitive to the location of the close relative to the high and low of the day. The 1-day stochastic is an excellent substitute for price when a (single-smoothed) 300-day *EMA* is taken, $SMI(1,300,1)$. Double smoothing provides smooth and timely indications of price. Applications of the 1-day stochastic include day trading, where the trader does not hold a position overnight. When opening gaps are present, close-to-close indicators such as the True Strength Index, or the *MACD*, will register the gap and affect the response curve for many subsequent bars from the opening. The 1-day stochastic is unaffected by the opening gap and thus is an excellent tool for the day trader.

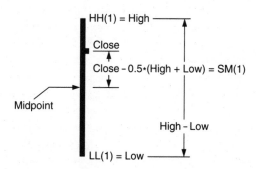

Figure 3–20 One-Day Stochastic

4

TICK VOLUME
INDICATOR

Tick data is a continuous stream of prices representing all transactions between buyers and sellers. It gets its name from the ticker tape. Within a specified time interval, the number of transactions may be large or small depending on market activity. And, market activity may be defined in terms of the volume of ticks. A particular transaction is considered to be an uptick if its price is higher than the price of the preceding transaction. Similarly, if the price of a transaction is lower than its preceding transaction, it is defined as a downtick. If all the ticks are up (all prices are always higher in a 20-minute interval), the close of the high-low bar will most certainly be at the high. Generally, this is not the case, and in any particular interval, the tick volume will be split between upticks and downticks.

Indicating the frequency of upticks and downticks *within* the high-low bar, or time period, is useful information for the day trader. The problem is gaps at the opening for intraday markets. For example, an indicator based on the close will register a strong reaction to an opening gap since the close for the previous day is largely displaced from today's close of the opening bar. The gap will bias the indicator response for a substantial period of time preventing a real assessment of the market during this period.

TICK VOLUME INDICATOR

Let us devise an indicator for day trading that separates the upticks and downticks in each price bar interval. (Upticks and downticks are available as direct intraday data using Omega Research's computer program for traders, *TradeStation,* for example). Let us define *DEMA*(upticks,*r,s*) as the *double (EMA) smoothing of the upticks.* By this, we first perform an exponential moving average of the upticks for *r*-bars; the result of the first smoothing is then exponentially smoothed for *s*-bars. Similarly, we define *DEMA*(downticks,*r,s*) as the *double (EMA) smoothing of the downticks.*

We then define the *Tick Volume Indicator (TVI)* as

$$TVI(r,s) = 100 \ \frac{DEMA(\text{upticks},r,s) - DEMA(\text{downticks},r,s)}{DEMA(\text{upticks},r,s) + DEMA(\text{downticks},r,s)}$$

which has a range from -100 to $+100$. (Note: An alternate definition that produces similar results may be made by taking the double *EMA* of the difference between the upticks and downticks in the numerator with the double *EMA* of the sum in the denominator.)

An example is shown in Figure 4–1 for an Omega Research continuous contract for the Deutsche mark with 20-minute bars. The second panel down shows *TVI* for double smoothing of 12 and 12 bars. The third panel down is for a slower *TVI* with double smoothing of 25 and 13 bars.

We immediately note the large down opening gaps at *A* and *B*. At *A*, prices are rising before and after the gap. Examination of *TVI* before and after the gap shows it is also rising before and after the gap. A similar situation exists at gap *B*. *TVI ignores the gaps entirely.* The Tick Volume Indicator *(TVI)* is a useful proxy for prices for the day trader.

Ergodic_TVI Oscillator

A particularly useful form of the *TVI* for day traders is the Ergodic_*TVI* oscillator patterned after the Ergodic oscillator of the True Strength Index. It consists of two parts: the oscillator and its Signal Line:

$$\text{Ergodic\_}TVI(r) = TVI(r,5)$$

$$\text{SignalLine}(r) = \text{EMA}(TVI(r,5),5).$$

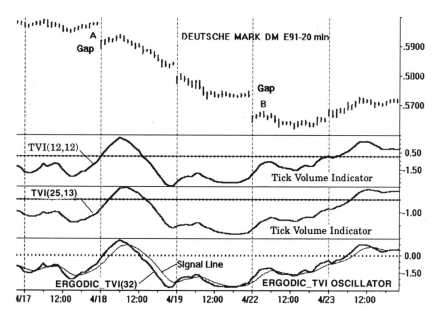

Figure 4-1 Tick Volume Indicator

The Ergodic_TVI is the double-smoothed TVI with one EMA smoothing fixed at 5 price bars. A further EMA smoothing of 5 price bars produces its Signal Line. This is shown in the bottom panel of Figure 4–1 for an EMA smoothing of r = 32 price bars. Note that the Ergodic_TVI(32) approximates TVI(12,12) and its Signal Line approximates TVI(25,13).

The two-part oscillator provides a convenient crossover system for day trading. Trading is performed in the direction of the trend. For example, assuming the trend direction has been determined to be down on April 18, a short entry can be made when the Ergodic crosses down under its Signal Line just prior to 12:00 noon. The trade is completed by an up crossover at the end of the day.

5

A DETRENDING
INDICATOR

Up to this point, we have devised double-smoothed indicators based on price alone (the close, for example)—the True Strength Index; then a family of indicators based on the high, low and close—the Stochastic Momentum Index; and lastly, a day trading indicator based on the tick volume—the Tick Volume Indicator (*TVI*). All of these indicators are smooth and timely since they are based on the principles of double smoothing, and they are essentially momentum indicators, (they are determined by comparing price levels at different times).

Other useful indicators are based on comparative differences. In this chapter, we shall present a double-smoothed indicator based on detrending.

DETREND

A trend may be defined in terms of a moving average. If the moving average of the close is rising, we say the market is on an uptrend. The moving average is smooth and introduces lag, which is evident at

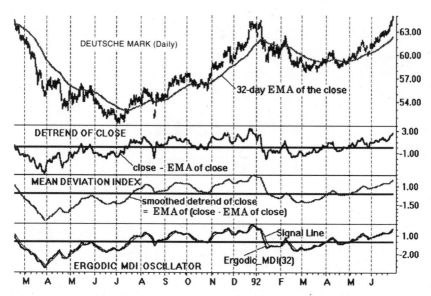

Figure 5–1 Close Detrend and Mean Deviation Index

turning points based on prices. A technique called "detrending" may be applied in which the moving average is subtracted from the close. This deviation

$$close - EMA(close, r)$$

is then plotted in lieu of the close (see second panel down of Figure 5–1 shown with an $r = 32$-day exponential moving average). The curve is observed to be jagged in appearance. To remove the noise, the detrended close is smoothed in the third panel down by an amount equal to $s = 12$-days. *Double smoothing* has been performed to obtain the clean curve.

MEAN DEVIATION INDEX

Let us *define* an indicator

$$MDI(close, r, s) = EMA(close - EMA(close, r), s)$$

called the Mean Deviation Index, *MDI*, using two moving averages. The first smoothing is of the close for r-days. The price series is detrended by subtraction of the moving average from the close. A second moving average for *s*-days is performed on the deviation; hence, the name, Mean Deviation Index. This is shown in the third panel of Figure 5–1 where the detrended close is smoothed an amount sufficient to produce a smooth and timely curve.

MACD APPROXIMATION

Under certain conditions, the *MDI* and the *MACD* (moving average convergence divergence) indicators approximate each other rather well. For example, when the double smoothing consists of one long interval, *r,* and a short interval, *s,* then

$$MDI(\text{close},r,s) \cong EMA(\text{close}, s) - EMA(\text{close}, r)$$

which is the definition of the *MACD*. It can be shown that *except for a scale factor,* the *MDI* and *MACD* have almost interchangeable shapes. As the intervals approach each other, the *MACD* becomes very small in amplitude. The basic double smoothing format, however, is in the formulation of the *MDI,* which accepts all values of *r* and *s*.

THE ERGODIC *MDI* OSCILLATOR

An ergodic format useful as a trading tool is possible with the Mean Deviation Index. This is shown in the bottom panel of Figure 5–1 consisting of an *Ergodic_MDI* oscillator and its *Signal Line:*

$$\text{Ergodic\_}MDI(r) = MDI(\text{close},r,5)$$

$$\text{Signal Line}(r) = EMA(MDI(\text{close},r,5), 5)$$

The ergodic *MDI* is the double-smoothed *MDI* with one of the smoothings fixed at 5 price bars. The signal line is a moving average of the ergodic *MDI* for 5 price bars. The amount of smoothing to obtain the signal line may be adjusted to suit. Usually, 3 to 12 price bars of smoothing are used. We use 5 price bars here.

Trading with the Ergodic_MDI Oscillator

The Ergodic *MDI* oscillator with its Signal Line provides a convenient means of trading on a close-to-close basis. An example is shown in Figure 5–2 for daily *T-bonds.*

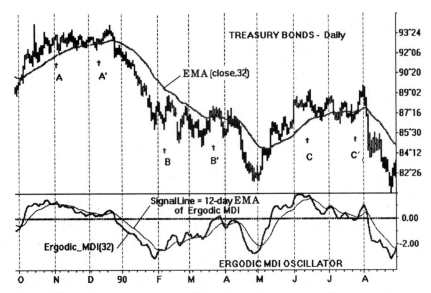

Figure 5–2 Trading with the Ergodic *MDI* Oscillator

A 32-day *EMA* of the close, *EMA*(close,32), defines the trend. A 32-day Ergodic *MDI*, *Ergodic_MDI*(32), is used as the trading instrument with a Signal Line assigned as a *12*-day *EMA* of the Ergodic *MDI*: SignalLine(32) = *EMA(MDI*(close,32,5),12).

Observation of the prices shows there are potential hazards for trading manifested by the three congestion regions: November–December 1989, February–March 1990, June–July 1990. Otherwise, prices trend very nicely having the potential for successful trading. We observe that the signal line is relatively smooth due to its 12-day smoothing interval and further that the slope of the signal line is in the same direction as the slope of the moving average on the close when prices are trending. In the congestion regions between points *A* and *A′, B* and *B′,* and *C* and *C′,* the slope of the signal line diverges from the slope of the moving average on the close: *The slopes are in opposition.* This *slope divergence* tells us that we are in a trading range, a region of congestion. With this knowledge, we may opt to exit a trade if we are holding one, or to stand aside and not trade if we are trend followers. On the other hand, it also permits us to exercise countertrend trading methods. The important item is that a *slope divergence* (see also Chapter 12) tells us we are entering or within a congestion region of prices.

When the Signal Line is going in the same direction as the trend defined by the 32-day *EMA* on the close, prices are trending and we should be alert for trading opportunities. For example, using a crossover philosophy, the Ergodic *MDI* crosses below its Signal Line following the slope divergence of the interval from A to A'. This occurs in late December 1989 and continues on a long decline for the month of January 1990 ending in the start of the slope divergence from B to B'.

The completion of the trading range from B to B' heralds the next down move in mid-April, which is entered by the Ergodic *MDI* crossing below its Signal Line. A long signal occurs in early May and exits at the beginning of a slope divergence (trading range) at C.

THE ERGODIC *MACD* OSCILLATOR

The *MACD* is similar to the mean deviation index, *MDI*. Both indicators are double-smoothed momentum indicators. We would expect that the *MACD* would also have an ergodic representation. The *MACD* is given by the difference between two exponential moving averages of the close:

$$MACD(\text{close},r,s) = EMA(\text{close},s) - EMA(\text{close},r)$$

where $EMA(\text{close},s)$ is the *EMA* of the close for s-days, and $EMA(\text{close},r)$ is the *EMA* of the close for r-days, with s less than r.

The Ergodic *MACD* then becomes

$$\text{Ergodic\_}MACD(r) = MACD(\text{close},r,5)$$
$$= EMA(\text{close},5) - EMA(\text{close},r)$$

and its Signal Line is represented by

$$\text{SignalLine}(r) = EMA(MACD(\text{close},r,5),5)$$

which is a 5-day *EMA* of the Ergodic *MACD*. The curves reproduce those of the *MDI* within a scale factor.

6

CANDLESTICK MOMENTUM

Candlestick charting is a chart representation used in Japan to describe prices. Since its recent introduction in the West, the subject has appeared in many articles, and in computer trading programs.

In lieu of a bar chart described by the open, high, low, and close, using a single vertical line, the candlestick chart is much more colorful and informative. The Japanese have developed a structure of pattern recognition inclusive of price reversals, or rally/decline terminations, and chart continuation patterns. These patterns are couched in a language peculiar to the history and lore of Japanese trading that developed over hundreds of years. Great emphasis is placed on the "real body" of the price bar, the portion of the price bar between the close and the open. The "shadows," the portions of the price bar outside of the real body, hold a secondary position in candle hierarchy.

Our interest in candlestick momentum is prompted by the effect of gaps on price charts on momentum indicators based on the close only (e.g., the *MACD* and *TSI*). The problem is significant in day trading, which is subject to frequent gaps in the opening price bar compared with the previous closing price bar. A large opening gap biases the *MACD*, or *TSI*, in its direction although prices may actually be progressing in the other direction. The erroneous information from the gap must be taken into account until the gap effect subsides.

In this chapter, a comparison is made between traditional charting and candlestick charting in terms of momentum. We shall show that *for intraday trading* the indicators based on candlestick momentum produce curves comparable to those of indicators based on close only momentum—with one major exception: *Candlestick momentum removes the bias due to gap effect.* Day traders using the candlestick indicators in this chapter may trade without the worry of opening gaps biasing their indicator readings.

MOMENTUM

Generally speaking, momentum is the slope of the curve describing the price phenomenon. A positive momentum corresponds to a price rise; conversely, negative momentum represents a price decline.

In technical analysis of stocks and commodities, momentum is classically defined as the current price (typically, the close) minus the price one time interval ago (e.g., today's close minus yesterday's close) although it can refer to the price difference over any time interval. With candlestick charts, the price bar is formed over a fixed time interval specified by the opening price, *open,* and the closing price, *close.* The change in price over this fixed interval is a momentum that I call the *candlestick momentum:*

$$cmtm = close - open$$

The *cmtm* can be plus or minus in the sense that an up momentum is positive when the close is greater than the open; the reverse is true when the open is greater than the close giving a negative value to the downward momentum.

CANDLESTICK MOMENTUM INDEX

Since candlestick momentum is a bona fide momentum in accordance with our definition, it is anticipated that methods of classical technical analysis momentum should be directly applicable. Following the method developed for the True Strength Index in Chapter 2, a *Candlestick Momentum Index (CMI)* can be constructed along the same lines:

$$CMI(\text{close,open},r,s) = 100 \; \frac{EMA(EMA(\text{cmtm},r),s)}{EMA(EMA(|\text{cmtm}|,r),s)}$$

The vertical bars in the denominator specify the *absolute value,* the positive value of the close − open momentum. Double smoothing is used in both the numerator and denominator to obtain smooth contours (low noise) with low lag. *EMA(cmtm,r)* is the first exponential moving average (*EMA*) of *r* price bars; this result is again smoothed for *s* bars by the second exponential moving average, *EMA(EMA(cmtm,r),s)*. The numerator by itself is double-smoothed candlestick momentum. The denominator performs the function of amplitude normalization, forcing the *CMI* to range from +100 to −100.

The *CMI* formula has the same format as the True Strength Index (*TSI*) and produces results *similar* to it. The maximum and minimum values of the *CMI* are 100 and −100, respectively. Prices are said to be overbought when the *CMI* is above a set threshold based on historical data; the oversold condition is attributed to prices when the *CMI* is less than a set negative threshold. Because the Candlestick Momentum Index uses differences, it will have many of the properties of other differencing indicators such as divergences, highlighting of price tops and bottoms, support and resistance, and trend lines. Price bar highs and lows do not enter into consideration for the *CMI,* only the close and open.

CANDLESTICK INDICATOR

An alternate formula using candlestick momentum is the *Candlestick Indicator (CSI),* which I have defined as

$$CSI(\text{close,open},r,s) = 100 \; \frac{EMA(EMA(\text{close-open},r),s)}{EMA(EMA(\text{high-low},r),s)}$$

This formula is more intuitive since we can visualize the close and open that define the limits of the candlestick graph along the price bar bounded by the high and low. In the numerator, an exponential moving average is taken of the close-open for *r* price bars. A second *EMA* is taken of this result for *s* price bars. A similar double smoothing is made in the denominator of the high-low price range of the bar. It is evident that the *CSI* ranges over +100 and −100. The value +100 is reached when the close is at the extreme point, the high, *and* the open occurs at the low. When the converse happens, the *CSI* will produce −100.

Figures 6–1 and 6–2 compare the *CSI* and *TSI* on S&P 500 futures 20-minute charts. Both the *CSI* and *TSI* are shown for double smoothings of 32 bars for each *EMA* smoothing. In Figure 6–1, the Candlestick Indicator based on the close-open momentum and the True Strength Index based on close-to-close momentum produce comparable results. Both rise and fall together and have near identical turning points. It appears either indicator can essentially be used interchangeably—*on intraday charts.* The interchangeability cannot always be made on daily charts.

Figure 6–2 is another time segment of the SP E91 (Omega Research continuous data S&P 500) 20-minute intraday chart. Three gap openings are present: two down gaps and one gap up. Prices following the down gaps continue lower in this example; both the Candlestick Indicator and the True Strength Index also decline.

The gap up represents a different situation. Prior to the gap, prices are declining. Immediately following the up gap, prices continue to decline. Except for the gap, a falloff in prices is present before and after the opening. The Candlestick Indicator registers this fact

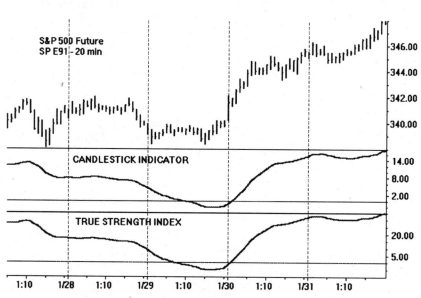

Figure 6–1   Candlestick Indicator and True Strength Index

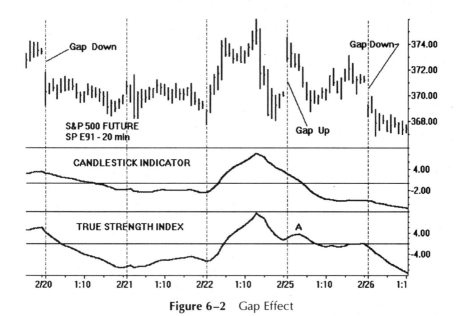

Figure 6–2 Gap Effect

exactly permitting the day trader to immediately take action: The bias of the opening gap is ignored entirely. The direction of prices (except for the gap) is preserved by the Candlestick Indicator.

The effect of the gap is not avoided by the True Strength Index, which faithfully records the close-to-close amplitude of prices. Although the gap occurs for one price bar, its effect provides an erroneous reading of prices as shown at point A.

ERGODIC CANDLESTICK OSCILLATOR

A good tool for the day trader is the ergodic oscillator using the Candlestick Indicator, *CSI*. It consists of two parts, the oscillator and its Signal Line:

$$\text{Ergodic\_CSI}(r) = CSI(\text{close,open},r,5)$$

$$\text{SignalLine}(r) = EMA(\text{Ergodic–}CSI(r),5).$$

The Ergodic *CSI* is the double-smoothed *CSI* with one *EMA* smoothing fixed at 5 price bars. A further smoothing of 5 price bars produces

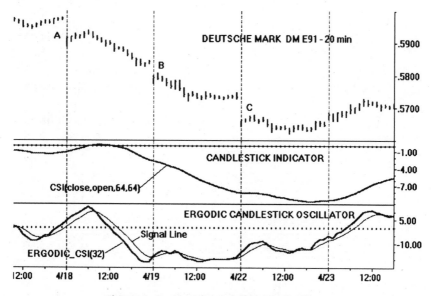

Figure 6–3   Ergodic Candlestick Oscillator

its Signal Line. This is shown in the bottom panel of Figure 6–3 for an *EMA* smoothing of $r = 32$ price bars. The oscillator is unaffected by the opening gaps, *A, B, C.* Therefore, all regions of the price bar are unbiased and are available for day trading. A slowly varying *CSI* in the middle panel of Figure 6–3 shows the direction of the trend. The Ergodic oscillator permits entry points that should be taken only in the direction of the trend.

7

DIRECTIONAL
TRENDING

One of the primary objectives of the investor/trader is to determine the direction of the market. Is it going generally up, or is it going down? Is the trend up, or down? If it is going up and we are comfortable that it is on a steady rise, we simply buy and hold; at a later time, we sell. It seems so easy to buy low and sell high. Why are we not all billionaires?

The markets do not always cooperate with the precepts of order and simplicity. Just when we feel comfortable and start counting our (paper) profits, the market whipsaws. Is this a real reversal? Are we entering a region of congestion, a narrow trading range? Should we get out? Is this just a minor variation in the ongoing trend? Then again, how much drawdown in equity should we tolerate if we decide to hold this position? Perhaps we should take our profits and get out? Should we cut our losses quickly? Depending on the situation, there are many possibilities. These are the familiar dilemmas of everyone who trades.

In this chapter, we shall attempt to quantify trending, directional movement, in terms of the highs and lows in the price bar graph. Starting with a momentum definition suitable for the highs and lows (the close is not used), a double-smoothed indicator is developed. Characteristics of the indicator relative to the bar graph are investigated to evaluate the existence of trends.

COMPOSITE HIGH-LOW MOMENTUM

Directional movement up, or upward trending, is first seen as a high of the price bar. The language of trading is replete with expressions such as "The rally began with an upside breakout of the high" and "The rally continues with day-to-day increasing highs." If the highs move up, increasing highs signify an uptrend.

Similarly, downtrends are first evidenced by the lows going lower. "The recent decline continues with lower lows appearing every day"; "The market had a late afternoon selloff with an avalanche of decreasing lows." In effect, lows moving to lower levels specify a downtrend, directional movement down.

The preceding word descriptions sound very much like momentum. An uptrend is positive direction with the amount of the upward change also specified. This sounds similar to the momentum of the high. The downtrend is in a down (negative) direction, and it is also specified with an amount. We recognize the downtrend word description as the momentum of the low.

We are in need of a different definition of momentum in this situation. The 1-day momentum of the close is given by *close today minus close yesterday*. The cumulative sum of this close momentum gives a curve that is, except for scaling, identical to the close.

What form may an appropriate momentum description have using *both* highs and lows? Let us *define* a composite high-low momentum as

$$HLM = \text{High\_}Mtm\text{\_Up} - \text{Low\_}Mtm\text{\_Down}$$

$$= HMU - LMD$$

where the upside momentum, *HMU*, is based solely on the highs, and the downside momentum, *LMD*, is calculated using only the lows. Only when the momentum of the highs is increasing is it used in the high-low momentum. Similarly, the momentum of the lows appears as *LMD* but only when it is decreasing. The upside momentum is calculated as follows:

If high[today] − high[yesterday] > 0 then

$$HMU = \text{high[today]} - \text{high[yesterday]}$$

Else

$$HMU = 0$$

Similarly, for the downside momentum:

If low[today] − low[yesterday] < 0 then

$$LMD = -(\text{low[today]} - \text{low[yesterday]})$$

Else

$$LMD = 0$$

VIRTUAL CLOSE

When the cumulative sum is taken of the composite high-low momentum, a single curve is obtained. This curve represents both the highs and lows; it is termed the virtual close and is shown in Figure 7–1

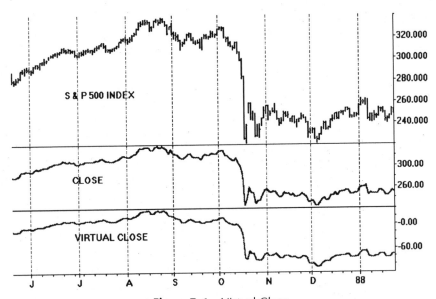

Figure 7–1 Virtual Close

compared with the actual close. It is evident that the virtual close and actual close track fairly well.

DIRECTIONAL TREND INDEX

The information for trending as defined by the increasing momentum of the highs in a rising trend and the decreasing momentum of the lows in a declining trend is embedded in the high-low momentum, *HLM*. In its raw form, it is very choppy with frequent changes from positive and negative values. Smoothing is required to make the information useful. Double smoothing is used in the definition of the Directional Trend Index (*DTI*) as

$$DTI(HLM,r,s) = 100\ \frac{EMA(EMA(HLM,r),s)}{EMA(EMA(\,|\,HLM\,|\,,r),s)}$$

where, for the numerator

$EMA(HLM,r)$ = exponential moving average of *HLM* for *r*-days

$EMA(EMA(HLM,r),s)$ = exponential moving average of $EMA(HLM,r)$ for *s*-days

and for the denominator

$EMA(\,|\,HLM\,|\,,r)$ = exponential moving average of the absolute value of *HLM* for *r*-days

$EMA(EMA(\,|\,HLM\,|\,,r),s)$ = exponential moving average of $EMA(\,|\,HLM\,|\,,r)$ for *s*-days

The numerator is the double exponential moving average of the high-low momentum, *HLM,* and the denominator is the double smoothing of its absolute magnitude, its positive value. In the numerator, the *HLM* is first smoothed for *r*-days. This result is smoothed with an *s*-day exponential. This is double smoothing of the numerator.

The Directional Trend Index presents characteristics that closely identify it with the True Strength Index given in Chapter 2. This is to be expected since it is a momentum indicator using the same algebraic format as the *TSI*. The *DTI* is double-sided in that it can vary

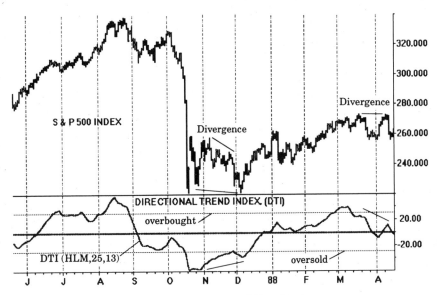

Figure 7–2 Directional Trend Index

over a range bracketed by +100 and −100. The *DTI* expresses over-bought and oversold price conditions and it highlights divergences between it and the price curve (specifically, the virtual close curve) from which it is derived. An example of the Directional Trend Index is given in Figure 7–2.

MEASURING DIRECTIONAL MOVEMENT WITH THE *DTI*

The *DTI* provides an excellent substitute for price. When the market goes up, the *DTI* goes up. There are times, however, when the *DTI* goes up although the market is in a trading range, or region of congestion. Similarly, when the market declines, the *DTI* also declines, but there are exceptions when the *DTI* declines during a market that is in congestion.

A study of many plots of the Directional Trend Index reveals its special characteristics for tracking trends. In the positive region of the *DTI* between zero and +100, a rising *DTI* corresponds to rising prices. A declining *DTI* in the positive region indicates falling prices *or* flat prices (a region of congestion); thus, the decreasing *DTI* provides an *ambiguous* indication of the direction of prices.

Similarly, in the negative region of the *DTI* between zero and −100, a decline corresponds to a decline in prices. However, an ambiguous situation again occurs for a rising *DTI,* which indicates *either* rising prices *or* flat prices.

Sideways movement of the indicator provides two additional possibilities, that is, a sideways movement of prices *or* transition in the gradual reversal of prices for all regions of the *DTI.*

Great care therefore must be exercised in the use of the indicator since it correctly identifies trends only under the following limited conditions:

- A positive price trend is uniquely identified by a rise occurring in the positive region of the *DTI* momentum indicator.

- A negative price trend is uniquely identified by a decline occurring in the negative region of the momentum indicator.

- All other regions of the momentum indicator are potentially erroneous.

These conditions are not unique to the DTI. *They prevail for indicators based on differences (momentum indicators).*

AMBIGUOUS INDICATIONS

The examples of Figures 7–3 and 7–4 demonstrate the ambiguous nature of the *DTI.* The stock *AMGEN* of Figure 7–3 is shown from August 1990 through December 1991 with a corresponding Directional Trend Index mostly in its positive region. From August to the end of October 1990, period *A,* the *DTI* has a negative slope, declining, and the corresponding prices are in a narrow trading range. The long price congestion region at *B* is also heralded by a negative slope of the *DTI.* Finally, at *C* the slope of the *DTI* is again negative but this time prices are also declining. In two cases, the negative slope showed congestion whereas in one case, the negative slope showed a downtrend. Had we assumed a downtrend in the first two cases and entered the market short, this would have resulted in a small loss. Positive slopes on the *DTI* in its positive region all made correct assessments of rising prices

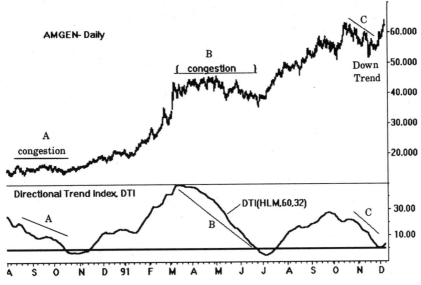

Figure 7–3 *DTI* Characteristics

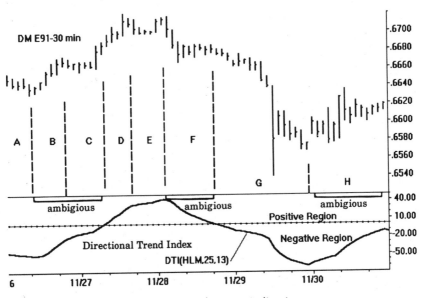

Figure 7–4 Ambiguous Indications

because of the one-to-one correspondence of the slopes of prices and the *DTI*.

Figure 7–4 is a plot of a half-hour bar graph of the Deutsche mark (an Omega Research continuous graph). This graph shows the possibilities in a momentum indicator such as the Directional Trend Index. The bottom panel contains the *DTI* above and below its zero line. In section *A*, the *DTI* is in its negative region and declining; prices in this section should also be uniquely declining—and they are. Except for the lag in sections *B* and *C*, the *DTI* is rising while in its negative region. This means that prices can be *either* rising *or* flat. It is observed that *B* is rising while *C* is flat. In this situation, the *DTI* could have been interpreted erroneously as *C* rising with *B* flat, which is seen to be patently incorrect.

Section *D* shows the indicator in its positive region rising sharply; prices in section *D* are also rising. The continued rally of the indicator in section *E* is shallow, almost flat. A sharp drop in the indicator all while in its positive region occurs in section *F* meaning that prices are *either* dropping *or* are in congestion; both of these conditions are present at different times in section *F*.

All of section *G* to November 30 is in a declining mode and occurs the negative region of the indicator. This uniquely defines a corresponding decline in prices that is observed to take place. Section *H* shows an increase in the indicator while it is in its negative region. This indicates one of two possibilities: a price rise, *or* flat prices. Here, observe a slow increase in prices.

TRADING WITH THE TREND

If we wish to follow trends with the intent of making money by buying or selling at different levels of the trend, it is essential that we know a trend is in effect. This is accomplished by smoothing prices, or smoothing of a momentum indicator of prices. Because smoothing prices directly has introduced lag, we have focused our attention on double smoothing of momentum indicators as surrogates of prices, which intrinsically have lower lag. We have seen in Figures 7–3 and 7–4 how the momentum indicator is a surrogate for price on a one-to-one basis only for specific regions; in other regions, it is an ambiguous surrogate, at best.

NONAMBIGUOUS TRENDING

If flat prices or frequent trading ranges occur, wrong trading decisions can be made when these decisions are based on momentum indicators. On the other hand, we can avoid many of the "wrong decisions" by following the indicators only under limited conditions. These conditions are

- Permit trading only when the indicator is increasing and is in its positive region.

- Permit trading only when the indicator is decreasing and is in its negative region.

These two conditions are the only ones that are assured to be nonambiguous.

An example of nonambiguous trending, called *DTI_Trade(25,13)*, is shown in the bottom panel of Figure 7–5. This notation specifies double smoothing in the Directional Trend Index of 25 and 13 bars, respectively, where only the indicator *rising in its positive region* and

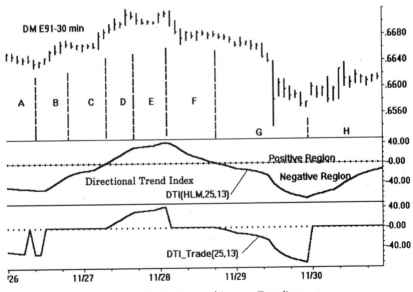

Figure 7–5 Nonambiguous Trending

falling it its negative region is retained. All other regions of the *DTI* are absent. This encompasses sections *A, D, E,* and *G* on the 30-minute bar graph. Trading will be permitted only in these sections because it is only in these sections that trending is uniquely defined as up or down (within the lag limitations of the indicator).

If a position is taken in sections *D* and *E,* it must be long since *DTI*_Trade is rising in these sections. Similarly, if it is decided to take a position in segment *G,* it must be short since the *DTI*_Trade indicator is falling.

Section *A* in Figure 7–5 showing the end of a decline also shows that the smoothing used was insufficient to prevent a return to zero caused by a single high-low bar having a noisy virtual close. This can be removed by using longer term smoothing—accepting the additional lag introduced by the additional smoothing.

A RUDIMENTARY TRADING VEHICLE

We now have the basic tools to construct a simple trading system—exclusive of money management. Our system will be based on *DTI*_Trade shown in the middle panel of Figure 7–6 and the Stochastic Momentum

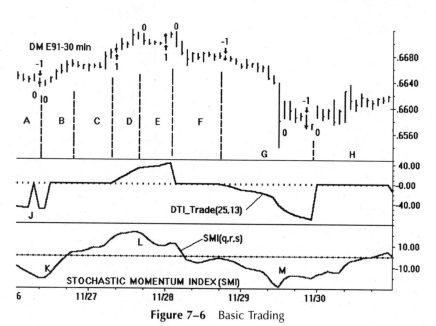

Figure 7–6 Basic Trading

Index, $SMI(q,r,s)$, in the lower panel operating as an oscillator. We will enter the market only when the $DTI\_$Trade indicator (middle panel) moves away from zero.

- Long entry occurs when $DTI\_$Trade goes positive. The position is held as long as the SMI oscillator (bottom panel) has the same slope going in the same direction as the trend shown in the middle panel of Figure 7–6.

- Long exit occurs when the slope of the SMI oscillator reverses such as at points L and M, or when $DTI\_$Trade returns to zero— whichever comes first

- Reentry. If the exit is based on a reversal of the oscillator, a reentry can be made when the oscillator turns again in the direction of the $DTI\_$Trade indicator; exit on the reentry follows the same rules as a standard exit.

Similar rules apply for short entry and exit.

This is shown in Figure 7–6 with the following notation: An up-arrow accompanied by a "1" signifies a long entry of one contract. A subsequent "0" indicates an exit from this long position. A down-arrow with a "-1" specifies a short entry of one contract. A "0" then indicates an exit from the short position.

Note that the noise at position J of the center panel produces a short entry that is immediately followed by a short exit one bar later. A similar situation occurs just prior to November 30. A long entry followed quickly by its exit occurs at November 28. These in-and-out trades are undesirable. They are the result of small noise variations and ever-present lag because of the averaging required to reduce these noise variations.

Smoothing improves results as shown in Figures 7–7 and 7–8. Figure 7–7 is a plot of the daily Deutsche mark with a Directional Trend Index with double smoothing of 20 days for each smoothing (middle panel). The portion of this curve that shows nonambiguous trending is directly below it and is seen to be very noisy. Faulty trades could be generated at positions A through K. With 5-day EMA smoothing of the DTI, potentially bad trades at positions A, B (maybe), C, D, F, H, and J are removed.

Nonambiguous trading is possible only when there are clear up-and-down patterns (ramps) in the $DTI\_$Trade. If the duration of a ramp

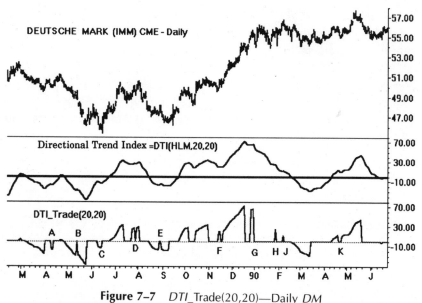

Figure 7–7 *DTI*_Trade(20,20)—Daily *DM*

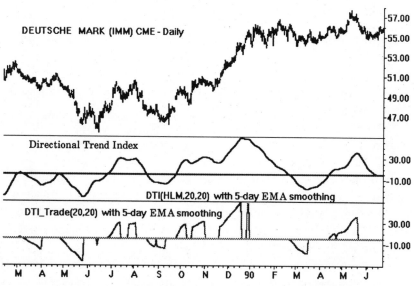

Figure 7–8 *DTI*_Trade(20,20) with 5-Day *EMA* Smoothing

is too short, or the ramp itself is not sufficiently steep, poor trading may result. In Figure 7–8, many of the *DTI*_Trade ramps are smooth and steep indicating that these regions are excellent for trading.

DTI_*Trade exists only for trends. It filters out trading ranges, congestion regions, and flat prices.* It performs this important function at the cost of some missed trading opportunities.

*DTI*_TRADE PERFORMANCE

Does trading using the *DTI*_Trade system work? The answer is yes. The answer is an *emphatic* yes if the market trends strongly and smoothly. *DTI*_Trade aids trading since it tends to prevent taking a position in trading ranges, congestion regions, or regions of flat prices. It identifies this category of prices as it occurs.

We may select markets that have a history of trending with the assumption that trending will continue into the future. Further, we may select a particular market and optimize it for best results on the recent past assuming the past data is likely to be similar in the future. These assumptions contain many difficulties: In the latter case, we can be rightly accused of curve-fitting the past, which will almost always produce stellar results . . . for the past. There is no one best way to "optimize."

Since we are attempting to show performance under limited conditions, we will set forth the following ground rules in this chapter:

- Daily Deutsche mark and daily T-bonds are compared using double smoothing of 28 days each with an additional 5-day smoothing to reduce noise.

- Both markets are further filtered by a smoothed Stochastic Momentum Index, *SMI(q,r,s)*, where the filtering is identical in all cases.

- Commission cost per trade is $20.

- Slippage cost per trade is $60.

- The performance is based on one contract traded.

- The performance summaries of Figures 7–9 through 7–12 are based on Omega Research's *Easy Language* and produced using the *TradeStation* computer program.

```
DTIwSMI DEUTSCHEMARK  06/92-Daily 06/30/82 - 06/30/92

                   Performance Summary:  All Trades

Total net profit        $12237.50   Open position P/L      $  4125.00
Gross profit            $62642.50   Gross loss             $-50405.00

Total # of trades             110   Percent profitable          49 %
Number winning trades          54   Number losing trades         56

Largest winning trade   $ 5057.50   Largest losing trade   $ -2480.00
Average winning trade   $ 1160.05   Average losing trade   $  -900.09
Ratio avg win/avg loss       1.29   Avg trade (win & loss) $   111.25

Max consec. winners             5   Max consec. losers            6
Avg # bars in winners          12   Avg # bars in losers          5

Max intraday drawdown   $-9902.50
Profit factor                1.24   Max # contracts held          1
Account size required   $12902.50   Return on account           95 %
```

Figure 7-9 Deutsche Mark (Daily): 10-Year Performance

```
DTIwSMI DEUTSCHEMARK  06/92-Daily 02/13/75 - 06/30/92

                   Performance Summary:  All Trades

Total net profit        $ 37962.50  Open position P/L      $  4125.00
Gross profit            $108217.50  Gross loss             $-70255.00

Total # of trades             195   Percent profitable          46 %
Number winning trades          89   Number losing trades        106

Largest winning trade   $ 8682.50   Largest losing trade   $ -2480.00
Average winning trade   $ 1215.93   Average losing trade   $  -662.78
Ratio avg win/avg loss       1.83   Avg trade (win & loss) $   194.68

Max consec. winners             5   Max consec. losers            6
Avg # bars in winners          12   Avg # bars in losers          5

Max intraday drawdown   $ -9902.50
Profit factor                1.54   Max # contracts held          1
Account size required   $ 12902.50  Return on account          294 %
```

Figure 7-10 Deutsche Mark (Daily): 17-Year Performance

```
DTIwSMI TREASURY BONDS 06/92-Daily 06/30/82 - 06/30/92

                   Performance Summary:  All Trades

Total net profit        $  3678.75  Open position P/L      $   500.00
Gross profit            $ 72788.75  Gross loss             $-69110.00

Total # of trades             113   Percent profitable          41 %
Number winning trades          46   Number losing trades         67

Largest winning trade   $ 5888.75   Largest losing trade   $ -4205.00
Average winning trade   $ 1582.36   Average losing trade   $ -1031.49
Ratio avg win/avg loss       1.53   Avg trade (win & loss) $    32.56

Max consec. winners             6   Max consec. losers            6
Avg # bars in winners          12   Avg # bars in losers          4

Max intraday drawdown   $-15657.50
Profit factor                1.05   Max # contracts held          1
Account size required   $ 18657.50  Return on account           20 %
```

Figure 7-11 T-Bond (Daily): 10-Year Performance

```
DTIwSMI TREASURY BONDS 06/92-Daily 09/21/77 - 06/30/92

                     Performance Summary:  All Trades

Total net profit       $ 20605.00   Open position P/L      $    500.00
Gross profit           $119187.50   Gross loss             $-98582.50

Total # of trades            169    Percent profitable         44 %
Number winning trades         75    Number losing trades        94

Largest winning trade  $  9263.75   Largest losing trade   $ -4205.00
Average winning trade  $  1589.17   Average losing trade   $ -1048.75
Ratio avg win/avg loss      1.52    Avg trade (win & loss) $   121.92

Max consec. winners            6    Max consec. losers           6
Avg # bars in winners         12    Avg # bars in losers         4

Max intraday drawdown  $-15657.50
Profit factor               1.21    Max # contracts held         1
Account size required  $ 18657.50   Return on account         110 %
```

Figure 7–12 T-Bond (Daily): 15-Year Performance

A visual examination of daily DM and T-bonds long-term charts will show that they are both trending markets. The DM trends better and smoother; consequently, we would expect to obtain better performance from the DM. According to the *TradeStation* program, the performance summary of Figure 7–9 for the daily Deutsche mark produces a total net profit of $12,237 in 10 years using 110 trades over this period, or roughly one trade, on average, per month. Half the trades were profitable; winning and losing trades were split almost equally. The intraday drawdown over the 10-year period was −$9,902; with a $3,000 margin required to trade the account, the account size required was $12,902 producing a return on the account of 95%. Not earth shaking, but nonetheless profitable at an average of 9.5% per annum considering that no attempt was made to systematically optimize. The 28-day double smoothing was selected because it produced visually smooth curves.

Trading was then performed on the DM for 17 years inclusive of the preceding 10-year interval. All other conditions remained unchanged. The trading net profit tripled to $37,962 using the same account size; the return on the account also tripled. The tripled numbers occurred by extending the trading vista backward by only 7 years. The DM was trending to a greater degree and much smoother in those early years. Examination of the DM price chart confirms this.

Figure 7–11 shows the trading results for one Treasury bond contract over the same 10-year period as the DM with all conditions held the same, inclusive of commission and slippage costs. The net profit was only $3,678 producing a return on the account of 20%, or 2% per year, on average. Performance over the 15-year interval that contains the 10-year interval is greatly enhanced as depicted in Figure 7–12. Total net profit increased better than fivefold. The account return also increased better than fivefold averaging better than 7% per year. Once again, the additional 5-year interval contained improved trending with less noise: fewer and longer successful trades. T-bonds results are not as good as the Deutsche mark since they are not as trending. Recent declines in performance are due to less trendiness than in earlier years.

SINGLE-SIDED, DOUBLE-SMOOTHED INDICATORS

Up to this juncture, the *HLM* was defined on a daily basis and then double smoothing was applied. Scaling was obtained using a denominator resulting in a bipolar (plus and minus) Directional Trend Index. It was then determined that a rising *DTI* in its plus region *uniquely* corresponded to rising prices; similarly, a falling *DTI* in its minus region *uniquely* corresponded to falling prices. All other possibilities were *ambiguous and potentially erroneous*. The *DTI*_Trade curve retained only the singular conditions of the *DTI* and made all other regions equal to zero. The zero regions excluded congestion regions and flat regions of prices. The zero regions also excluded some regions of price trends—missed trading opportunities.

Other forms of processing the *HLM* are possible. For example, we may take the (double-sided) *DTI* and compute its absolute value, or we may double-smooth the *HLM* in following the procedure:

1. Single-smooth the *HLM*.

2. Take the absolute value of (1).

3. Smooth the absolute value.

This method of double smoothing is used in Wilder's *ADX*, and described in Appendix A. We shall identify this smoothing sequence as an *ADX*-type double smoothing.

ABSOLUTE VALUE OF THE *DTI*

The Directional Trend Index with double smoothings of 32 days each is shown for the daily Deutsche mark in the middle panel of Figure

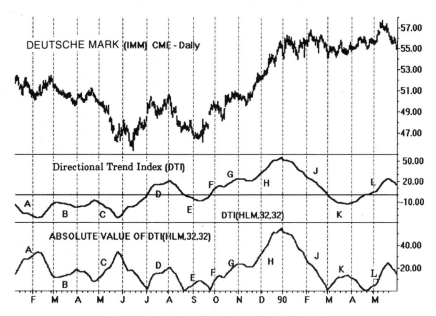

Figure 7-13 Absolute Value of the *DTI*

7-13. It appears to be relatively smooth and timely. The lower panel of Figure 7-13 is the absolute value of the *DTI*. The absolute value of the double-smoothed momentum indicator provides a method for separating price trends from flat prices and congestion regions. Positive regions of the *DTI* are unchanged by the absolute value. Negative regions, however, are folded over into the positive region. Negative slopes in the negative region are folded over into the positive region appearing as positive slopes. Positive slopes in the negative region become negative slopes in the positive region by using the absolute value.

Positive slopes on the absolute value of the *DTI* correspond to trending. Negative slopes on the absolute value of the *DTI* correspond to *either* price flats, congestion regions, *or* price trends. By confining trades to the positive slopes of the absolute magnitude, we will avoid price regions of little or no directional movement, which can be hazardous for trading. There will be times, however, when this technique rejects trends that are perfectly suitable for trading.

Negative slopes in the negative region of the *DTI* (middle panel of Figure 7-13) include segments *A, B, C, E,* and *K* which have positive slopes in the absolute value of the *DTI* (bottom panel). Positive slopes in the positive region of the *DTI* include segments *D, F, G, H,* and L which also have positive slopes in the absolute value to the *DTI*. All of these segments have positive slopes in the absolute value and *uniquely* identify *either* rising *or* falling prices, directional movement. The *direction of prices is lost in the absolute value* and must be found by other available means, such as a moving average. Negative slopes on the absolute value of the *DTI* are potentially erroneous as seen by the trading range indicated in the segment *J*.

No new information is gained by taking the absolute value of the *DTI*. The ability to identify unique rising *or* falling prices is preserved by observation of rising slopes. The ability to determine *direction* without outside assistance is lost, however. The *DTI*_Trade formulation is preferred because it provides both uniqueness and direction.

ADX-TYPE DOUBLE SMOOTHING

Pre- and post-smoothing of the absolute value of the *HLM* is shown in the bottom panel of Figure 7–14. This is *ADX*-type double smoothing

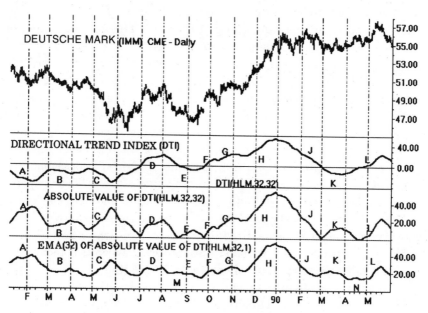

Figure 7–14 Pre- and Postsmoothing of Absolute Value of *DTI*

as previously described, (see also Appendix A). It is observed to be *similar* in appearance to the absolute value of the *DTI*. Closer examination reveals the differences between the two. Following LeBeau and Lucas, we consider a trend to be in force when the slope is positive, the curve is rising. We will make comparisons with the absolute value of the *DTI*, also shown in Figure 7–14. The *DTI*, which is also plotted, will be used to show direction.

Segment *A* is rising, a directional movement that is seen in the *DTI* to be declining prices. (Remember: The absolute value destroys information on direction.) Segment *B* is a rise in *DTI* absolute value corresponding to a downtrend in prices. The *ADX*-type filter is flat in the *B* segment indicating no directional movement, a missed opportunity to trade. Segment *C* is a sharp downturn in prices which is indicated by rising curves.

Segment *D* is a fast double top in prices. The *DTI* processing does not detect the double top although it does indicate that the segment is tradable because of its positive slope. The *ADX*-type processing attempts, within its lag limitations, to track the double top using two small segments of positive slope.

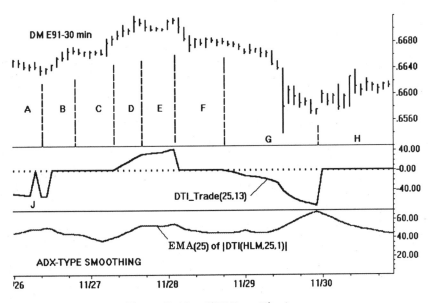

Figure 7–15 *ADX*-Type Filtering

Segment *E* on the *DTI* processing correctly shows a decline in prices by its rising curve. The *ADX*-type filtering disagrees showing a falling curve, a possible missed opportunity to trade. Segments *F, G, H, K,* and *L* are in agreement identifying possible trading (trending) opportunities.

Figure 7–15 displays both *DTI*_Trade filtering and *ADX*-type filtering using the same smoothing times for 30-minute day trading. Using the strategy of trading opportunity only for positive slope of the *ADX*-type filter, and stand aside or exit for negative slopes, both forms of filtering are comparable. Again in this example, the *ADX*-type filter is slightly more sensitive to variations in the price curve.

It is not possible at this point to make a declaration as to which form of processing is "better." They both produce comparable, yet different results.

8

TRUE STRENGTH
DIRECTIONAL TRENDING

We have shown how directional movement is defined in terms of the highs and lows. Leaning on the intuitive reasoning that increasing highs go with an uptrend and decreasing lows go with a downtrend, we defined an indicator based on a high-low momentum that measured trending. Trending, the directional movement of prices, was tied directly to the definition of momentum.

This raises a very important question: If momentum is basic to directional movement, are other indicators available to measure trending based on other definitions of momentum?

In this chapter, we explore the use of the True Strength Index (*TSI*), introduced in Chapter 2, as a momentum trading vehicle based on the close (or the high, or the low) only.

MEASURING DIRECTIONAL MOVEMENT
USING THE TRUE STRENGTH INDEX

An extensive review of many plots of the *TSI* and the close curves from which they are derived show that the indicator is loaded with potentially erroneous data. In the technical analysis of stocks and commodities, the compelling reason for using momentum indicators is the lower lag these indicators exhibit. Prices are noisy and require smoothing. Smoothing of price is accompanied by lagging response. Using momentum, the lag is significantly reduced and many of the momentum characteristics are helpful in trading: Overbought, oversold data are available and divergences are present that are not available in the price alone.

Momentum indicators, however, are potentially flawed because they can provide ambiguous signals. When the *TSI* momentum indicator (using the closing price) is between zero and +100, a rising *TSI* (increasing one-bar momentum) corresponds to rising closes. A falling *TSI* is identified with two possible price conditions: falling prices *or* flat prices.

A similar situation exists for the *TSI* while it ranges from 0 to −100 where a falling *TSI* corresponds to falling prices. However, a rising *TSI* in this region can provide two possible interpretations: rising prices or flat prices.

An example is shown in Figure 8–1. From mid-January 1991 to mid-February, the *TSI* (above zero) rises with rising prices. From

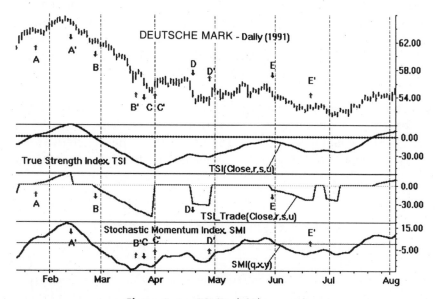

Figure 8–1 *TSI*_Trade(Close,*r,s,u*)

mid-February to the end of the month, the *TSI* (still above zero) declines with falling prices. The *TSI* correctly identified falling prices in this case although a falling *TSI* in the positive region can also occur for flat prices. The month of March shows the *TSI* declining while in its negative region specifying a one-to-one correspondence with falling prices. Next, from the beginning of April, the *TSI* remains in its negative region and is on a rise; however, prices remain flat. This is one of the two possible conditions indicated by a rising *TSI* while in its negative region. This situation occurs again for the entire month of May.

Fast price changes are not always correctly specified by the *TSI* because of inherent lag. There is always a delay in the response. When the *TSI* is created using slower moving averages, it has a larger lag. The presence of some lag is an unavoidable problem for any analysis based on smoothing.

The True Strength Index in Figure 8–1 is used with three levels of smoothing for the daily Deutsche mark: $r = 32$ days, $s = 13$ days, and $u = 3$ days. Normally, we use double smoothing of r and s days. However, a third level of smoothing for a small number of days is applied here to remove small but rapid fluctuations. The small number of days in the smoothing process does not add appreciably to the lag.

TSI_TRADE FILTER

We want to trade using the *TSI* as a trend indicator. We wish to have an indicator that shows prices trending in the direction of the indicator. A rising trend in the indicator corresponds uniquely with increasing prices; a falling indicator corresponds one-to-one with falling prices. We define *TSI*_Trade(close,r,s,u) to accomplish this. It is exactly the *TSI*(close,r,s,u) that exists in those regions. At all other times, it is made equal to zero. This is shown in Figure 8–1.

A BASIC TRADING SYSTEM

Think of the *TSI*_Trade curve as a filter. Whatever passes the filter can then be traded using any strategy. For example, consider using an indicator such as the Stochastic Momentum Index (*SMI*) of Chapter 3 as a trading instrument as shown in the bottom panel of Figure 8–1. The following rules are listed:

Long Positions

- Enter long when *TSI*_Trade rises above zero and the slopes of *TSI*_Trade and the *SMI* are both positive.

- Exit long when *SMI* slope turns negative or when *TSI*_Trade reverts back to zero, whichever comes first.

Short Positions

- Enter short when *TSI*_Trade declines below zero and the slopes of *TSI*_Trade and the *SMI* are both negative.

- Exit short when *SMI* slope turns positive or when *TSI*_Trade reverts back to zero, whichever comes first.

CAUTION: *This is not intended to be a complete trading system. It is included here to demonstrate principles only.*

Starting in late January, a long entry occurs at point *A* (see Figure 8–1) and an exit is caused by the *SMI* slope reversal at *A'*. We then stand aside. Toward the latter part of February, a short position is taken at point *B;* the position is held for the fall in prices until the exit at point *B'*. Because of a wiggle of the *SMI,* another short entry is made at point *C* of the March falloff; the exit was taken due to the simultaneous *SMI* reversal and *TSI*_Trade revert to zero.

We stand aside for the flat prices in early to mid-April. A short position is held from points *D* to *D'*. This is not a good trade because of the lag. The trade was indicated properly, but too late. It is not a costly trade. May is a poor month for trading; *TSI*_Trade filter has us stand aside. Next, we enter a short at *E* at the end of May and exit the position at *E'* due to a reversal of the *SMI* slope.

9

STOCHASTIC TRADE FILTERING

Directional trending was accomplished in the previous chapter using the True Strength Index (*TSI*). In this chapter, we shall briefly describe the use of the Stochastic Momentum Index (*SMI*) for directional trending. The reader will find a description of the *SMI* and its double-smoothed properties in Chapter 3. We shall use a version of the Stochastic Momentum Index, *SMI(q,r,s,u)*, in which q is the look-back period, r and s are *EMA* smoothing increments. An additional smoothing of u bars is used when needed to remove high-frequency noise.

MEASURING DIRECTIONAL MOVEMENT WITH THE STOCHASTIC MOMENTUM INDEX

Like all other momentum indicators, the *SMI* can provide erroneous signals. The *SMI* is defined over a range from $+100$ to -100. When it is rising and is above zero, it correctly identifies a rising trend (after a delay or lag has taken place). Similarly, when it is falling and is below zero, there is a one-to-one correspondence between the *SMI* and the declining price. All other conditions are *potentially* incorrect. For example, when the *SMI* is falling and in its positive region, it is indicative of two possible conditions: (1) falling prices, or (2) flat prices. When the *SMI* is rising and the rise takes place in its negative region, it indicates two possible conditions: (1) rising prices, or (2) flat prices.

Our objective is to identify clear, unambiguous trends. To accomplish this identification, we do not use all portions of the Stochastic Momentum Index, *SMI(q,r,s,u)*. We only use that portion which rises while in the positive region, or that portion which falls while in its negative region. All other regions are declared to be equal to zero. This defines *SMI_Trade(q,r,s,u)* as shown in Figure 9–1.

The complete *SMI(q,r,s,u)* is also shown in Figure 9–1. It has a period of $q = 32$ days which is *EMA*-smoothed by $r = 64$ days. These two parameters define double stochastic smoothing. An additional smoothing of $s = 7$ days is applied to remove most of the high-frequency fluctuations. The u parameter performs no smoothing function here and is set equal to 1. It is observed that the *SMI* has both rising and falling segments.

From January 1990 on through March 1990, prices are more or less flat, in congestion. We wish to identify this region, or at minimum

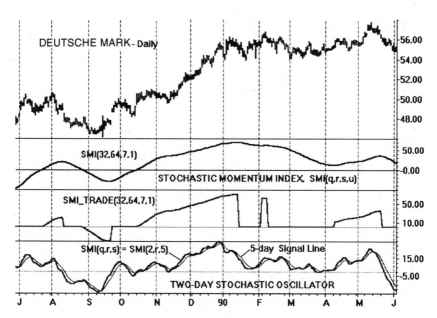

Figure 9–1   *SMI*_Trade Filter

to stand aside. During this interval, the *SMI* is falling, which could lead to an erroneous interpretation that prices are also falling. This is avoided entirely by the definition of the *SMI*_Trade*(q,r,s,u)* shown in Figure 9–1.

The bottom panel shows the 2-day stochastic oscillator, described in Chapter 3, which is used to identify turning points which are passed by the *SMI*_Trade filter. Only those regions of the *SMI*_Trade filter that are nonzero may be considered. This eliminates the need for trading for most of the congestion period.

*SMI_*TRADE MODES

The *SMI* used here has four parameters: *q,r,s,u*. Only three are required to describe the various *SMI* operating modes. The fourth is included for noise cleanup and is usually a small number to prevent adding appreciable lag. Any two parameters define an *SMI* operating mode. Modes are defined (bold print) as:

1. SMI(**q,r**,*s*,1). *s* is used for noise cleanup.

2. SMI(2,**r,s**,*u*). *u* is used for noise cleanup.

3. SMI(1,**r,s**,*u*). *u* is used for noise cleanup.

The various modes are shown in Figure 9–2 for the same-valued parameters.

The *SMI*_Trade filtering is somewhat different for each of the modes. The (**q,r**,*s*,1) mode is the second panel down. It passes the mid-October to mid-January trend (although the first month of this trend is flat). The congestion starting in mid-January is correctly avoided except for a spike in early February. We say that the *SMI*_Trade filter has "rejected" the congestion since it is zero.

By comparison, the (2,**r,s**,*u*) mode identifies the rally from mid-November to mid-January during its strongest rise. During the following congestion, two spike are present.

Finally, mode 3 (1,**r,s**,*u*) is shown in the fourth lower panel.

Regardless of the mode used, *SMI*_Trade acts as a prefilter for the fast-acting entry/exit oscillator that is a part of the trading system. It tends to prevent trading during regions of price congestion, trading ranges. In performance of this valuable function, it can miss

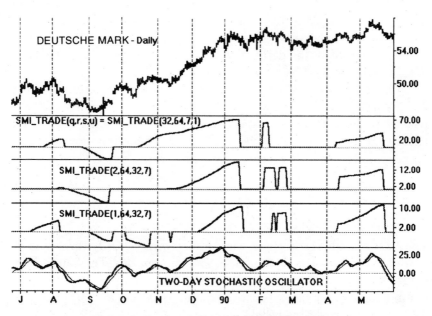

Figure 9–2 Comparison of *SMI*_Trade Modes

trends and does not permit action on them; it can therefore miss trading opportunities.

Trade entry depends on *both* SMI_Trade and the *SMI(q,r,s,u)* oscillator. For example, the spikes in Figure 9–2 would not be entered long because the *SMI* oscillator in February 1990 is in an overbought condition.

10

*TVI*_TRADE
FILTERING

In Chapter 4, we defined an indicator based on the upticks and
downticks occurring during the formation of a high-low price bar. The
Tick Volume Indicator (*TVI*) was especially useful since it was unaffected by gaps. This property makes it a prime candidate for intraday
trading application where opening gaps occur often. These gaps bias
the response of many other indicators and, in so doing, prevent trading until the gap effects disappear.

DIRECTIONAL MOVEMENT WITH
THE TICK VOLUME INDICATOR

All momentum-type indicators can show erroneous information. This
is also the case for the Tick Volume Indicator of Chapter 4. Examination of the indicator over many price applications shows that trends
are indicated without ambiguity (within lag constraints) when the indicator is rising and is positive (a rising trend), and when the indicator is falling and is negative (a declining trend).

Our aim is to use the *TVI* as an indicator of trends and to either avoid or identify flat prices and congestion regions. An example is shown in Figure 10–1 for the S&P 500 continuous contract (Omega Research method) with 60-minute bars. The Tick Volume Indicator is shown with three levels of smoothing: $TVI(r,s,u) = TVI(32,32,5)$. The third level of smoothing of 5 bars is included to help in high-frequency noise cleanup.

The third panel depicts $TVI\_Trade(r,s,u) = TVI\_Trade(32,32,5)$. When *TVI* is rising and is in its positive region or when *TVI* is falling and is in its negative region, then *TVI*_Trade and *TVI* are equal; for all other situations, *TVI*_Trade is equal to zero.

A BASIC *TVI* INTRADAY TRADING SYSTEM

Consider *TVI*_Trade as a filter. When it is zero, trading is not permitted. When it exists sloping upward, long positions may be taken and completed. Similarly, when it is sloping downward, short positions my be entered and exited.

In the bottom panel of Figure 10–1, a *TVI* oscillator is used as a trading instrument. We are permitted entry only in the direction of

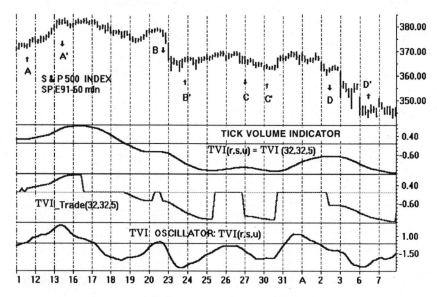

Figure 10–1 *TVI*_Trade Filter

the *TVI*_Trade trend; exit is expressed as oscillator reversal from the trend.

   CAUTION: This is not intended to be a complete trading system. It is included here to demonstrate principles only.

   Rules for entry and exit are as follows:

Long Positions

- Enter long when *TVI*_Trade rises above zero and the slopes of *TVI*_Trade and the *TVI* oscillator are both positive.

- Exit long when the *TVI* oscillator slope turns negative or when *TVI*_Trade reverts back to zero, whichever comes first.

Short Positions

- Enter short when *TVI*_Trade declines below zero and the slopes of *TVI*_Trade and the *TVI* oscillator are both negative.

- Exit short when the *TVI* oscillator slope turns positive or when *TVI*_Trade reverts back to zero, whichever comes first.

The *TVI* oscillator has 3 levels of smoothing in this example. The third level is used for noise cleanup. Typically, it will be a small value, from 2 to 5 price bars, and does not add appreciable lag to its turning points.

   The first trade shown is a long entry at point *A*. Both *TVI*_Trade and the *TVI* oscillator have positive slope at this point. The trade exits at point *A'* due to a reversal of slope of the *TVI* oscillator. Although the *TVI*_Trade filter continues on with its positive slope, further entry is not permitted since the oscillator has an opposing (negative) slope.

   On day 19, *TVI*_Trade shows a downward slope opening the gate for short trading. Trade entry is not permitted, however, since the *TVI* oscillator slope is in opposition; it is positive.

   The next opportunity by *TVI*_Trade occurs on the latter part of day 20. A short entry is made at point *B* since both slopes are negative, going down. The short position exits at point *B'* when the oscillator reverses slope. Trade from *C* to *C'* and from *D* to *D'* are completed in similar fashion. Note that the gap did not affect trade from *D* to *D'*.

11

ADX-TYPE FILTERING

In Appendix A, an attempt is made to reproduce the substance and flavor of Wilder's *ADX,* an indicator intended to measure and use directional movement. The process uses double smoothing where the first smoothing involves functions of the highs and lows, the *DI Diff* and *DI Sum* (Wilder's notation). At this point, the absolute value of the process is taken resulting in the *DX,* or Directional Movement Index. Finally, a second moving average is taken of the *DX* resulting in the *ADX,* or average directional movement. In Chapter 7, under the heading *ADX*-Type Double Smoothing, the process was introduced for the high-low momentum, *HLM.*

This very unusual process of double smoothing forms the basis of a class of filtering which we will call an *ADX*-Type Filter, or by the acronym, *ATF.*

THE *ATF* PROCESS

The object of the *ATF* process is to construct filters that detect trends and directional movement, and reject or identify congestion regions of prices. It is intended to be a filter that is applied prior to the trader's "usual" processing strategy. The following basic steps are applicable:

1. Select a single-smoothed, double-sided momentum indicator as a trading instrument.

2. Take the absolute value of the indicator of Step 1.

3. Single-smooth Step 2.

4. Trends are deemed to exist only for positive slopes found in Step 3.

We shall apply this process using the example of Figure 11–1 for the daily Deutsche mark. The second panel down is a plot of the *ATF* filter. The third panel is the True Strength Index (*TSI*), from which it is derived. The fourth panel is *TSI*_Trade of Chapter 8 used for comparison.

Starting with Step 1, the single-smoothed, bipolar, momentum indicator selected here is the True Strength Index, $TSI(close,r,s) = TSI(close,32,1)$. The *TSI* formula is for double smoothing of r- and s-days. By letting $r = 32$ and $s = 1$, the formula represents single smoothing of 32-days.

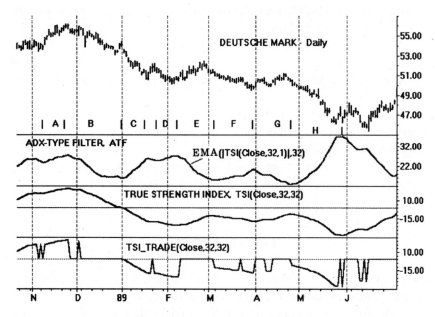

Figure 11–1 The *ATF* Process with the *TSI*

With Step 2, the absolute value of the *TSI* is $|TSI(\text{close},32,1)|$, where vertical bars enclosing the single-smoothed *TSI* are the notation for absolute value.

Step 3 requires single-smoothing of the absolute value of the *TSI* of Step 2. This result is the definition of *TSI_ADX*-Type Filter, *TSI_ATF*:

$$TSI\_ATF(\text{Close},32,32) = EMA(|TSI(\text{close},32,1)|,32)$$

where $EMA(|TSI(\text{close},32,1)|,32)$ is the 32-day exponential moving average of the absolute value of the 32-day single-smoothed *TSI*.

The effect of performing the absolute value is to take negative values of the single-smoothed *TSI* and fold them over into the positive scale bounded by 0 and +100. The effect takes negative slopes from the negative region and transforms them into positive slopes in the positive region. Single-smoothing of this result brings us to Step 4 of the process. Trends are identified by this process; the direction of the trends, however, are not indicated.

AMBIGUOUS INDICATIONS

Let us trace the *ATF* of Figure 11–1 viewing its positive slopes separately from its negative slopes. At the same time, we will compare it with the double-smoothed *TSI* and the *TSI*_Trade using the same parameters.

In segments *A, C, D, F,* and *H,* the slope of the *ATF* is positive, a rising *ATF*. This correctly indicates the directional movement as trending. In segment *A,* the trend is up. In segments *C, D, F,* and *H,* prices are going down. This is corroborated by *TSI*_Trade(close,32,32), which also shows direction. In segments *B, E,* and *G,* the slope of the *ATF* is negative. These correspond to zero regions of the *TSI*_Trade. Negative slopes of the *ATF* do not always mean a congestion region is present in prices. Segment *B* shows a price decline. Segment *E* indicates a price advance. Segment *G* shows flat prices. The negative slope of the *ATF* can be easily interpreted erroneously. Trending is uniquely indicated only for positive slopes of the *ATF*. The *direction* of the trending, however, is not indicated by the *ATF*. Direction must be obtained from sources such as a momentum indicator or a moving average.

AN *ATF* FILTER USING STOCHASTIC MOMENTUM

We repeat the *ATF* process selecting the Stochastic Momentum Index, *SMI(q,r,s)* = *SMI*(32,1,1) as shown in Figure 11–2. The *SMI* formula is for double smoothing when any two of the *q,r,s* parameters are selected. In this example, we set the look-back interval at $q = 32$ with $r = s = 1$; the formula then represents single smoothing of 32 days.

Next we obtain the absolute value of the single-smoothed *SMI* as $|SMI(32,1,1)|$. Note again the meaning of the vertical bars as the absolute value of that enclosed between the bars.

Next we perform single-smoothing of the absolute value. This result is the definition of the *SMI_ADX*-Type Filter, the *SMI_ATF*:

$$SMI\_ATF(32,32) = EMA(|SMI(32,1,1)|, 32)$$

where $EMA(|SMI(32,1,1)|, 32)$ is the 32-day exponential moving average of the absolute value of the 32-day (look-back) single-smoothed stochastic momentum index (*SMI*).

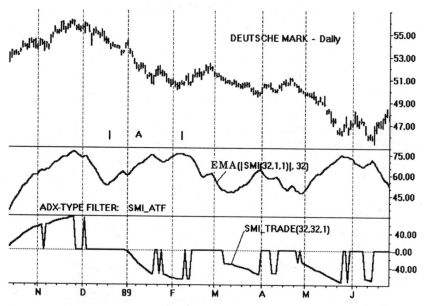

Figure 11–2 The *ATF* Process Using Stochastic Momentum

This brings us to step 4 of the *ATF* process where we examine only the positive slopes of the *SMI_ATF* for trends. Comparison is made with $SMI\_\text{Trade}(q,r,s) = SMI\_\text{Trade}(32,32,1)$ and differences do occur in filtering. See segment *A*, for example, where the *ATF* has a positive slope indicating trending well before it occurred in its corresponding *SMI*_Trade.

12

SLOPE
DIVERGENCE

We have used various forms of prefiltering with the objective of separating price trends from regions of congestion. The techniques all used double smoothing of bipolar momentum indicators, in other words, momentum indicators whose values fluctuate from positive to negative. To isolate regions of congestion, trends were identified only in those regions of the indicator which were rising and positive, or were falling and negative. Other regions of the momentum indicators were potentially erroneous indicating either congestion or trends. Although this procedure uniquely identified trends (within lag limitations), it did not pick out all the trends that were present. There were many missed opportunities.

Ideally, we are in search of a technique that directly isolates the congestion regions, those regions of flat prices. If we can do this, all other regions will be trends, which is what we seek as trend followers.

SLOPE DIVERGENCE

Two ingredients are required to directly identify "flat" prices: (1) a moving average of prices, and (2) a bipolar momentum indicator of prices based on moving average(s) of momentum. The technique is best explained by examples.

Figure 2–9 (Anatomy of a Rally: Price and Momentum) in Chapter 2 is an idealized figure showing a price rally at A followed by a region of flat prices at B. A moving average of the rally and its subsequent flat region is shown to be constantly rising. A momentum description appears in the bottom half of the Figure 2–9. For the rally at A, the momentum is flat and the moving average of momentum is rising together with the moving average of prices. For the flat region of B, the momentum is zero and the moving average of momentum decays to zero while the moving average of prices continues to rise. In the region of flat prices, the slope of the moving average of prices and the slope of the moving average of the momentum of prices are in opposite directions—we have a *slope divergence* situation.

By contrast, trending requires the moving average of momentum to be going in the same direction as the moving average of prices. If we define a trend by its moving average on its price, then the maxim, "go with the trend," is exemplified by the direction of the slopes relative to each other. We go with the trend when the slopes are in the same direction. We stand aside, or use countertrend trading techniques, when the slopes are in opposition, or *divergent*.

An example of the slope divergence technique is shown in Figure 12–1 for AMGEN and its long rally terminating in the congestion of prices of March and April 1991. On the top panel, the bar chart is shown with an overlay of a 32-day *EMA* of the close, *EMA*(close,32). The *EMA* rises with the rally and continues its rise through the flat congestion region. In the second panel, a plot of the *TSI*(close,r,s) = *TSI*(close,32,32) is used as the bipolar momentum indicator. Double smoothing of 32 days each is used. It is observed that the *TSI* tracks the rally: Its slope follows that of the moving average of price when prices are rising and goes in opposition when prices oppose the moving average. In early to mid-January, there are flat prices. In this region, the moving average (*EMA*) continues its rally up; however, slope divergence is present since the *TSI* is going down.

SLOPE DIVERGENCE *TSI* FILTER

The bottom panel of Figure 12–1 is a single plot of the slope divergence technique. It is the same as the *TSI* of the middle panel with the

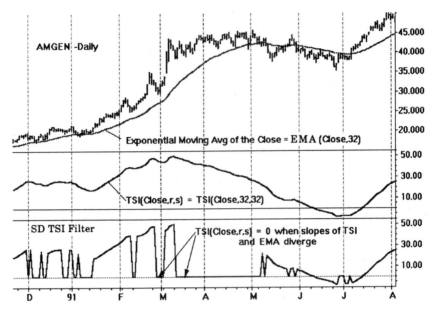

Figure 12–1 Slope Divergence

exception that it goes to zero whenever slope divergence exists. It is nonzero whenever slope divergence is absent; it is nonzero whenever trending exists. Limitations from this ideal once again are imposed by ever-present *lag* and price fluctuations not in tune with the moving average periods used in the momentum indicator.

We define a slope divergence filter using the True Strength Index (*TSI*) as *SD_TSI*(close,*r*,*s*,*u*,*x*,*y*). In this notation, a triple-smoothed *TSI*(close,*r*,*s*,*u*) is used with sequential exponential moving averages of *r, s,* and *u* time intervals, respectively. In addition, a double exponential moving average is used as the moving average on price. Thus, sequential exponential moving averages of *x* and *y* intervals are evaluated on the close. In this way, the bottom panel of Figure 12–1 is expressed as *SD_TSI*(close,32,32,1,32,1). The technique is depicted with double smoothing of 32 days each in the *TSI* since *u* = 1. In addition, since *y* = 1 single smoothing of 32 days is applied to the close.

Are these parameters apropos for AMGEN? They appear to be timely: Wherever there is a flat region in prices, or a changeover from rising to falling prices (and vice versa), the *SD_TSI* filter goes to zero in a timely fashion. In other regions where prices are trending, the

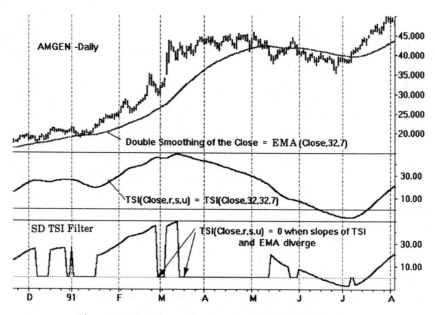

Figure 12–2 Slope Divergence: Additional Smoothing

SD_TSI filter also trends in the same direction. The problem, however, is the noisiness, which could be harmful in a trading system.

Additional smoothing is needed to clean up the high-frequency noise variation, as shown in Figure 12–2. A third level of smoothing where $u = 7$ days is used in the *TSI*. Also a second level of smoothing with $y = 7$ days is applied to the close. With these values, the *SD_TSI* filter in the bottom panel is expressed as *SD_TSI*(close,32,32,7,32,7). The resulting response is cleaner and smoother but at a cost of additional *lag*. How much additional smoothing should be applied is a function of the trading system used with the *SD_TSI* filter and the volatility of prices.

A BASIC SLOPE DIVERGENCE *TSI* TRADING SYSTEM

Following the same approach used in Chapter 8 for *TSI*_Trade, we may consider the slope divergence technique based on the *SD_TSI* as a prefilter to our usual trading methods. Figure 12–3 illustrates this using the slope divergence method of Figure 12–1 as a prefilter for an indicator such as the Stochastic Momentum Index, *SMI*(*q,r,s*). We may

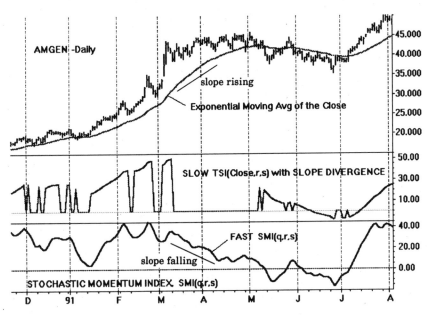

Figure 12–3 Basic Slope Divergence Trading System

think of the *SD_TSI* as a "slow *TSI*" which goes to zero for flat regions of prices. We may further think of this modulated slow *TSI* as a substitute for trending prices.

A fast-acting indicator, for example, a "fast *SMI*" is introduced in the bottom panel. This indicator is used for trading purposes to accompany the trend represented by the surrogate. We take a position when the slopes are in the same direction. We exit a position when slopes are in opposition.

SLOPE DIVERGENCE TECHNIQUE VERSUS *TSI*_TRADE

Ideally, the slope divergence technique would identify regions of price congestion, or flat prices. What remains would then be trends, either positive or negative. Does this actually happen? *TSI*_Trade identified trends but many escaped its view. Are these missed trading opportunities regained by the slope divergence technique? Again, the answer to these questions is unclear.

Consider the comparison of the *TSI*_Trade and *SD_TSI* plots of Figure 12–4 using the same moving average values. A fast-acting Sto-

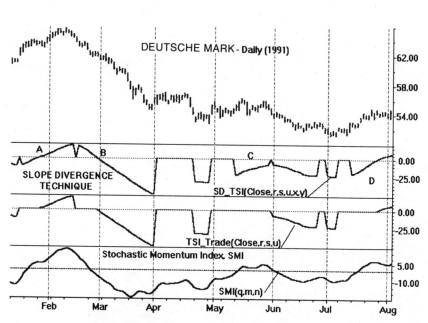

Figure 12–4 Slope Divergence versus *TSI* Trade

Stochastic Momentum Index *(SMI)* is used as the trading instrument after prefiltering. Note that slope divergence extends the time on the price rally for the segment at *A* compared with *TSI*_Trade. A similar situation exists at segment *B*. Slope divergence excels in this situation.

Consider segment *C*, which shows a minor fluctuation that may not be tradable. This is not a problem for *TSI*_Trade which is at zero negating the possibility of trading. Finally, segment *D* of the slope divergence method catches a small rally that is missed entirely by *TSI*_Trade.

SLOPE DIVERGENCE VERSUS PRICE DIVERGENCE

Figure 12–5 is a comparison of slope divergence and price divergence for the weekly Deutsche mark. Usually, the term divergence, when associated with a momentum indicator is a comparison of the indicator directly with its corresponding prices. Consider the price divergence *B*. The closing prices begin and end segment *B* at approximately the same level. The corresponding points on the *B* segment for the True Strength

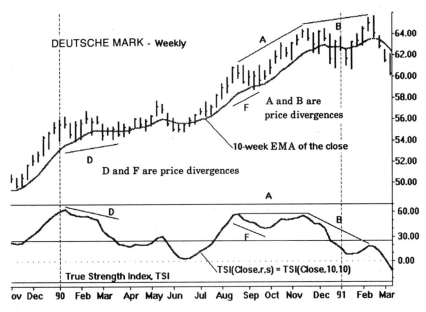

Figure 12–5   Price Divergence versus Slope Divergence

Index (*TSI*) do *not* have the same levels. The peaks are directed down. This divergence is termed a down-divergence indicating that subsequent prices will *likely* be lower. In this case, prices were lower.

Segment *A* also describes a downward divergence. Here the amplitude of prices is rising without a corresponding rise in the *TSI*. This is often followed by a flat region with another divergence such as at *B*. The resultant double divergence is construed to be a stronger indication of a trend change. Triple divergences (not shown) are even more powerful indications of trend change when they occur. Price divergences must be especially heeded when they occur near historically overbought or oversold regions as they did in Figure 12–5.

Slope divergence is different from price divergence. With slope divergence, a comparison is made of the *slope of the momentum indicator* and that of the *slope of the moving average of price*. When the slopes diverge, we usually will be in a region of flat prices, a congestion region. Unlike price divergences where we must wait for the second amplitude to signal the occurrence of a divergence, slope divergence is indicated without delay. This is exactly what happens at the slope divergences of segments *D* and *F*. Prices are rising and then enter a flat region. The moving average of price is also rising and continues to rise throughout the flat price region at *D*. The situation is entirely different for the *TSI* momentum indicator. As prices rise, the *TSI* also rises. However, immediately on entering the congestion region, the *TSI* quickly reverses direction, going down. The slopes of the *TSI* and the moving average of price are in opposition: A slope divergence is *in process* indicating flat prices are *in process*.

Appendix A

WILDER'S *ADX*

Many advances in the understanding of technical analysis occurred before the advent of the personal computer. One of the milestones was the publication by J. Welles Wilder in 1978 of *New Concepts in Technical Trading System* (see References). This book presented new indicators and trading techniques in spreadsheet form suitable for use with programmable calculators. This pioneering work of great stature has survived the test of time. Much of the content of this highly recommended book is still of prime value and in current use.

In this 1978 publication, Wilder said: "Directional movement is the most fascinating concept I have studied. Defining it is a little like chasing the end of a rainbow . . . you can see it, you know it's there, but the closer you get to it the more elusive it becomes." This feeling about directional movement persists today. Various investigators have tested Wilder's *DMI* techniques and their derivatives with varying degrees of success. The work of LeBeau and Lucas (see References) summarizes their own efforts and those of others.

Appendix A reviews in brief the *DMI* and *ADX* concepts of Wilder using his original notation as well as a method suggested by LeBeau and Lucas for using the *ADX*.

ADX FORMULA DERIVATION

According to Wilder, the basic increment of directional movement is the largest part of today's range that is outside of yesterday's range. Using Wilder's notation, this is shown in Figure A–1 for a rising market with a $+DM$, a falling market with a $-DM$, and an outside day having both a $+DM$ and a $-DM$ (the largest of the two is retained), and an inside day for which DM = 0 is assigned. The notation $+DM$ signifies a directional movement up, whereas a $-DM$ stands for a down directional movement.

Wilder defines the true range to describe volatility as the largest of

1. The *difference* between today's high and today's low,

2. The *difference* between today's high and yesterday's close, or

3. The *difference* between today's low and yesterday's close.

The true range, *TR,* is a positive number.

Next, the Directional Indicator is calculated as $DI = DM/TR$ where $+DI = +DM/TR$ represents the percentage of the true range that is up for the day, and $-DM/TR$ is the percentage that is down for the day. Note: the $+$ and $-$ signs are labels to indicate positive and negative directions, *not* addition and subtraction.

Next, the true range is averaged over the past 14 days to obtain TR_{14}. Then the average over the same period of $+DMs$ is taken to obtain $+DM_{14}$, and the average of the $-DMs$ over 14-days produces $-DM_{14}$. With these values, Wilder then calculates the average upward directional indicator, $+DI_{14} = +DM_{14}/TR_{14}$, and a corresponding average downward directional indicator, $-DI_{14} = -DM_{14}/TR_{14}$.

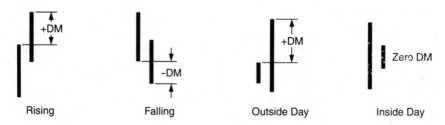

| Rising | Falling | Outside Day | Inside Day |

Figure A–1 One-Day Directional Movement

Referring to the spreadsheet on pages 41–42 of Wilder's book, the absolute value of the difference between the up- and down-average directional indicators is formed as $DI\ DIFF = |(+DI_{14}) - (-DI_{14})|$ where the vertical enclosing bars indicate the absolute, or positive value. The sum is also calculated as $DI\ SUM = (+DI_{14}) + (-DI_{14})$, which is a positive value. (Remember, the $+$ and $-$ *DIs* are labeled to indicate up and down directions, *not* addition and subtraction.)

Next, the *DX* or Directional Movement Index is defined by

$$DX = 100\ \frac{(DI\ DIFF)}{(DI\ SUM)}$$

which can take on values from zero to $+100$. The *DX* does not depend on the true range since it cancels out of the equation:

$$DX = 100\ \frac{|(+DM_{14}) - (-DM_{14})|}{(+DM_{14}) + (-DM_{14})}$$

Finally, the average directional movement, the *ADX*, is calculated by taking an average of the 14-day period of the *DX*:

$$ADX = DX_{14}.$$

In effect, the *ADX* uses a form of double smoothing.

INTERPRETATION

According to Wilder, the more directional the movement of a commodity or stock, the greater will be the difference between $+DI_{14}$ and $-DI_{14}$. You go *long* when $+DI_{14}$ crosses over $-DI_{14}$ and you go *short* when $-DI_{14}$ crosses over $-DI_{14}$. You only trade those markets that are high on a (positive only) *ADX* scale. Methods of trading are discussed, where the use of the *ADX* emphasizes amplitude.

LeBeau and Lucas review Wilder's work and that of others and conclude that the slope of the *ADX* is of greater importance than its level. A rising *ADX* indicates a strong trend is in process and that trend-following trading techniques should be used. They also conclude that a falling *ADX* indicates a trendless market and that countertrend strategies (such as overbought and oversold strategies) should be applied. No action is best if you favor trend following.

Appendix B

TRADESTATION™ AND SUPERCHARTS™ CODE

The graphs in this book were plotted using Omega TradeStation, a computer program for traders by Omega Research, Inc., in Miami, Florida. The code for the various charts is contained in this appendix. A TradeStation user may directly reproduce many of the charts. The appendix may be used as an entry to double-smoothed momentum indicators and their applications.

SuperCharts™ by Omega Research is another trading program that is compatible with TradeStation. Most of the code herein can be used on SuperCharts.

The code is described as *user function* code or *indicator* code. As defined by Omega, a function is a calculation, a formula for calculation. Many functions are built in the programs. Others such as those listed here must be devised by the user. Indicator code produces the graphs that are plots of market indicators, or market analysis. Functions are used in indicator code. A function could be a formula for a market index such as the True Strength Index. Essentially, a function is a formula assigned to a name. Using functions simplifies writing code and expressing indicators.

Figure B–1 is a User Function code named *TXAverage* for Triple Exponential Moving Average. The code appears in the format: *TX-Average*(Price,*r,s,u*) where an *r*-period moving average is performed on Price; an *s*-period moving average is then performed on the result of the first moving average; and finally, a *u*-period EMA is performed on the result of the first two moving averages. The actual code is in bold print.

The True Strength Index of Chapter 2 appears in Figure B–2 as a user function named *TSI*. Triple exponential smoothing is used in the code which calls up the *TXAverage* user function of Figure B–1.

The *Ergodic* is plotted from indicator code with two inputs. The default values of the inputs are shown within the closed parentheses. The input is an *r*-period of 32 with a fixed horizontal line at zero. There are three plots. Plot 1 is the user function formula for the True Strength Index. The plot is named "Ergodic." Plot 2 is a 5-period *EMA* of Plot 1 named the "SigLin." Plot 3 is simply a horizontal line at zero named "Zero."

The procedure for coding follows the method of the preceding examples.

USER FUNCTION

TXAverage

Code
/////////////

{User Function: TXAverage = Triple Exponential Moving Average

...by Bill Blau }

{FORMAT: TXAverage(Price, r, s, u) }

Inputs: **Price(NumericSeries), r(NumericSimple), s(NumericSimple),**

u(NumericSimple) ;

TXAverage = XAverage(XAverage(XAverage(Price,r),s),u) ;

Figure B–1   TXAverage: Triple *EMA*

USER FUNCTION

TSI

Code
///////////////

{ User Function: TSI = True Strength Index

by Bill Blau }

{ Triple exponential moving averages are used. }

{ FORMAT: TSI(Price, r, s, u)   }

Inputs: Price(NumericSeries), r(NumericSimple), s(NumericSimple),

u(NumericSimple);

Value1 = 100 * TXAverage(Price - Price[1], r, s, u) ; {Numerator}

Value2 = TXAverage(AbsValue(Price - Price[1]), r, s, u) ; {Denominator}

If Value2 < > 0 then

TSI = Value1 / Value2

Else

TSI = 0 ;

Figure B–2   *TSI:* True Strength Index

INDICATOR

Ergodic

Code
/////////////

{ Indicator: Ergodic

....by Bill Blau }

{ FORMAT: Ergodic(r)

SignalLine(r) }

Inputs: r(32), ZeroLine(0);

Value1 = TSI(Close, r, 5, 1) ;

Value2 = XAverage(TSI(Close, r, 5, 1), 5) ;

Plot1(Value1, "Ergodic") ;

Plot2(Value2, "SigLin") ;

Plot3(ZeroLine, "Zero") ;

Figure B-3 Ergodic Oscillator

USER FUNCTION

DI

Code
////////////////

{ User Function: DI = Divergence Indicator

(Numerator of the TSI)

by Bill Blau }

{ Triple exponential moving averages are used. }

{ FORMAT: DI(Price, r, s, u)   }

Inputs: Price(NumericSeries), r(NumericSimple), s(NumericSimple),

u(NumericSimple);

DI = 100 * TXAverage(Price - Price[1], r, s, u) ;

Figure B–4   *DI:* Divergence Indicator

USER FUNCTION

DS_Stochastic

Code
//////////////

```
{ User Function:    DS_Stochastic = Double-smoothed Stochastic

                        by  Bill Blau }

{ Double exponential moving averages are used. }


{ FORMAT:  DS_Stochastic(q,r,s)

                where q = lookback period

                    r = period of first EMA

                    s = period of second EMA  }

Inputs:      q(NumericSimple), r(NumericSimple), s(NumericSimple);


Value1 = XAverage(XAverage(Close - Lowest(Low,q),r),s) ;

Value2 = XAverage(XAverage(Highest(High,q) - Lowest(Low,q),r),s) ;

If Value2 < > 0 then

      Value3 = 100 * Value1 / Value2

Else

      Value3 = 0 ;

DS_Stochastic = Value3 ;
```

Figure B–5 *DS_Stochastic*

USER FUNCTION

DXAverage

Code
////////////////

{User Function: DXAverage = Double Exponential Moving Average

...by Bill Blau }

{FORMAT: DXAverage(Price, r, s) }

Inputs: Price(NumericSeries), r(NumericSimple), s(NumericSimple) ;

DXAverage = XAverage(XAverage(Price,r),s);

Figure B–6   DXAverage: Double *EMA*

USER FUNCTION

SM

Code
//////////////

```
{ User Function:    SM = Stochastic Momentum

                        by Bill Blau }

{ Double exponential moving averages are used. }

{ FORMAT:  SM(q,r,s)

                where q = lookback period

                    r = period of first EMA

                    s = period of second EMA  }

Inputs:      q(NumericSimple), r(NumericSimple), s(NumericSimple);

Value1 = 100 * DXAverage(C - 0.5 * (Highest(H,q) + Lowest(L,q)),r,s);

SM = Value1;

{where  C = Close,  H = High,  L = Low }
```

Figure B–7   *SM:* Stochastic Momentum

USER FUNCTION

SMI

Code
///////////////

{ User Function: SMI = Stochastic Momentum Index

by Bill Blau }

{ Double exponential moving averages are used. }

{ FORMAT: SMI(q,r,s)

where q = lookback period

r = period of first EMA

s = period of second EMA }

Inputs: **q(NumericSimple), r(NumericSimple), s(NumericSimple);**

Value1 = DXAverage(C - 0.5 * (Highest(H,q) + Lowest(L,q)),r,s) ;

Value2 = 0.5 * DXAverage(Highest(H,q) - Lowest(L,q),r,s) ;

If Value2 < > 0 then

Value3 = 100 * Value1 / Value2

Else

Value3 = 0 ;

SMI = Value3 ;

Figure B–8   *SMI:* Stochastic Momentum Index

USER FUNCTION

TVI

Code
/////////////

{ User Function: TVI = Tick Volume Indicator

by Bill Blau }

{ Double exponential moving averages are used. }

{ FORMAT: TVI(r,s)

where r = period of first EMA

s = period of second EMA }

Inputs: r(NumericSimple), s(NumericSimple);

Value1 = DXAverage(Upticks,r,s) ; {Double EMA smoothing of upticks}

Value2 = DXAverage(Downticks,r,s) ; {Double smoothing of downticks}

If Value1 + Value2 < > 0 then

TVI = 100 * (Value1 - Value2) / (Value1 + Value2)

Else

TVI = 0 ;

Figure B-9   *TVI:* Tick Volume Indicator

INDICATOR

Ergodic_TVI

Code
/////////////////

{ Indicator: Ergodic_TVI

....by Bill Blau }

{ FORMAT: Ergodic_TVI(r)

SignalLine(r) }

Inputs: r(32), ZeroLine(0);

Value1 = TVI(r, 5) ;

Value2 = XAverage(TVI(r, 5), 5) ;

Plot1(Value1, "ErgTVI") ;

Plot2(Value2, "SigLin") ;

Plot3(ZeroLine, "Zero") ;

Figure B–10   Ergodic_*TVI* Oscillator

USER FUNCTION

MDI

Code
///////////////

{ User Function: MDI = Mean Deviation Indicator

by Bill Blau }

{ FORMAT: MDI(Price, r, s, u) }

Inputs: **Price(NumericSeries), r(NumericSimple), s(NumericSimple), u(NumericSimple);**

MDI = XAverage(XAverage(Price - XAverage(Price,r),s),u) ;

Figure B–11 *MDI:* Mean Deviation Indicator

INDICATOR

Ergodic_MDI

Code
/////////////

{ Indicator: Ergodic_MDI

....by Bill Blau }

{ FORMAT: Ergodic_MDI(r)

SignalLine(r) }

Inputs: **r(32), ZeroLine(0);**

Value1 = MDI(Close, r, 5) ;

Value2 = XAverage(MDI(Close, r, 5), 5) ;

Plot1(Value1, "ErgMDI") ;

Plot2(Value2, "SigLin") ;

Plot3(ZeroLine, "Zero") ;

Figure B–12   Ergodic_*MDI* Oscillator

INDICATOR

Ergodic_MACD

Code
/////////////

{ Indicator: Ergodic_MACD

....by Bill Blau }

{ FORMAT: Ergodic_MACD(r)

SignalLine(r) }

Inputs: **r(32), ZeroLine(0);**

Value1 = MACD(Close, r, 5) ;

Value2 = XAverage(MACD(Close, r, 5), 5) ;

Plot1(Value1, "ErgMACD") ;

Plot2(Value2, "SigLin") ;

Plot3(ZeroLine, "Zero") ;

Figure B–13   Ergodic_MACD Oscillator

USER FUNCTION

CMI

Code
/////////////

{ User Function: CMI = Candlestick Momentum Index

by Bill Blau }

{ Triple exponential moving averages are used: r, s, u. For most applications,

double smoothing with u = 1 will be sufficient. }

{ FORMAT: CMI(r, s, u)   }

Inputs: r(NumericSimple), s(NumericSimple), u(NumericSimple);

Value1 = 100 * TXAverage(Close - Open, r, s, u) ; {Numerator}

Value2 = TXAverage(AbsValue(Close - Open), r, s, u) ; {Denominator}

If Value2 < > 0 then

    CMI = Value1 / Value2

Else

    CMI = 0 ;

Figure B–14   *CMI:* Candlestick Momentum Index

USER FUNCTION

CSI

Code
/////////////

{ User Function: CSI = CandleStick Indicator

by Bill Blau }

{ Triple exponential moving averages are used: r, s, u. For most applications,

double smoothing with u = 1 will be sufficient. }

{ FORMAT: CSI(r, s, u)   }

Inputs: **r(NumericSimple), s(NumericSimple), u(NumericSimple);**

Value1 = 100 * TXAverage(Close - Open, r, s, u) ; {Numerator}

Value2 = TXAverage(High - Low, r, s, u) ; {Denominator}

If Value2 < > 0 then

CSI = Value1 / Value2

Else

CSI = 0 ;

Figure B–15   *CSI:* CandleStick Indicator

INDICATOR

Ergodic_CSI

Code
/////////////

{ Indicator: Ergodic_CSI

....by Bill Blau }

{ FORMAT: Ergodic_CSI(r)

SignalLine(r) }

Inputs: **r(32), ZeroLine(0);**

Value1 = CSI(r, 5, 1) ;

Value2 = XAverage(CSI(r, 5, 1), 5) ;

Plot1(Value1, "ErgCSI") ;

Plot2(Value2, "SigLin") ;

Plot3(ZeroLine, "Zero") ;

Figure B–16 Ergodic_*CSI* Oscillator

USER FUNCTION

HMU

Code
/////////////

{ User Function: HMU = High Momentum Up

by Bill Blau }

{ Used in Directional Trend Index, DTI }

Condition1 = High - High[1] > 0; {rising high}

If Condition1 then

HMU = High - High[1]

Else

HMU = 0 ;

Figure B–17   *HMU:* High Momentum Up

USER FUNCTION

LMD

Code
/////////////

{ User Function: LMD = Low Momentum Down

by Bill Blau }

{ Used in Directional Trend Index, DTI }

Condition1 = Low - Low[1] < 0; {falling Low}

If Condition1 then

LMD = - (Low - Low[1])

Else

LMD = 0 ;

Figure B–18   *LMD:* Low Momentum Down

USER FUNCTION

DTI

Code
//////////////

{ User Function: DTI = Directiional Trend Index

by Bill Blau }

{ Triple exponential moving averages are used with periods of r, s, u. In many

cases, double smoothing will be sufficient in which case: u = 1 }

{ This user function deals with HLM = HMU - LMD. See user functions: HMU

and LMD}

{ FORMAT: DTI(r, s, u) }

Inputs: r(NumericSimple), s(NumericSimple), u(NumericSimple);

Value1 = 100 * TXAverage(HMU - LMD, r, s, u) ; {Numerator}

Value2 = TXAverage(AbsValue(HMU - LMD), r, s, u) ; {Denominator}

If Value2 < > 0 then

DTI = Value1 / Value2

Else

DTI = 0 ;

Figure B–19   *DTI:* Directional Trend Index

USER FUNCTION

DTI_Trade

Code
//////////////

{ User Function: DTI_Trade

by Bill Blau }

{ Triple exponential moving averages are used with periods of r, s, u. In many
 cases, double smoothing will be sufficient in which case: u = 1 }
{ The DTI is derived here. Only those portions of the DTI which are positive and
are rising are retained. In addition, only those portions which are negative and
falling are retained. The derivation is based on HLM = HMU - LMD where HMU
represents the increasing momentum of the high's and LMD is the decreasing
momentum of the low's}

{ FORMAT: DTI_Trade(r, s, u)   }

```
Inputs:      r(NumericSimple), s(NumericSimple), u(NumericSimple);

Value1 = 100 * TXAverage(HMU - LMD, r, s, u) ; {Numerator of DTI}
Value2 = TXAverage(AbsValue(HMU - LMD), r, s, u) ; {Denominator of DTI}

If  Value2 < > 0 then
      Value3 = Value1 / Value2
Else
      Value3 = 0 ;          { Value3 represents the DTI }
If Value3 - Value3[1] >0  AND Value3 > 0 then
      Value4 = Value3
Else                          {Value4 is that portion of the DTI which is positive
      Value4 = 0 ;              and rising}
If Value3 - Value3[1] <0  AND Value3 < 0 then
      Value5 = Value3
Else                          {Value5 is that portion of the DTI which is negative
      Value5 = 0 ;              and falling}
DTI_Trade = Value4 + Value5 ;
```

Figure B–20   *DTI*_Trade

USER FUNCTION

TSI_Trade

Code
/////////////

{ User Function: TSI_Trade = True Strength Index Trade

by Bill Blau }

{ Triple exponential moving averages are used. }

{ FORMAT: TSI_Trade(Price, r, s, u) }

Inputs: Price(NumericSeries), r(NumericSimple), s(NumericSimple),

u(NumericSimple);

```
Value1 = TSI(Price, r, s, u) ;

If Value1 - Value1[1] > 0 AND Value1 > 0 then
      Value2 = Value1
Else                          {Value2 is that portion of the TSI which is positive
      Value2 = 0;             and rising}

If Value1 - Value1[1] < 0 AND Value1 < 0 then
      Value3 = Value1
Else                          {Value3 is that portion of the TSI which is negative
      Value3 = 0 ;            and falling}
TSI_Trade = Value2 + Value3 ;
```

Figure B–21   *TSI*_Trade

USER FUNCTION

SMI_Trade

Code
////////////////

{ User Function: SMI_Trade = Stochastic Momentum Index Trade

by Bill Blau }

{ FORMAT: SMI_Trade(q, r, s) }

Inputs: q(NumericSimple), r(NumericSimple), s(NumericSimple) ;

Value1 = SMI(q, r, s) ;

If Value1 - Value1[1] > 0 AND Value1 > 0 then
      Value2 = Value1
Else   {Value2 is that portion of the SMI which is positive
      Value2 = 0;   and rising}

If Value1 - Value1[1] < 0 AND Value1 < 0 then
      Value3 = Value1
Else   {Value3 is that portion of the SMI which is negative
      Value3 = 0 ;   and falling}

SMI_Trade = Value2 + Value3 ;

Figure B–22   *SMI*_Trade

USER FUNCTION

TVI_Trade

Code
////////////////

{ User Function: TVI_Trade = Tick Volume Indicator Trade

by Bill Blau }

{Use only with Upticks and Downticks}

{ FORMAT: TVI_Trade(r, s) }

Inputs: **r(NumericSimple), s(NumericSimple) ;**

Value1 = TVI(r, s) ;

If Value1 - Value1[1] > 0 AND Value1 > 0 then
      Value2 = Value1
Else   {Value2 is that portion of the TVI which is positive
      Value2 = 0;   and rising}

If Value1 - Value1[1] < 0 AND Value1 < 0 then
      Value3 = Value1
Else   {Value3 is that portion of the TVI which is negative
      Value3 = 0 ;   and falling}

TVI_Trade = Value2 + Value3 ;

Figure B–23   *TVI*_Trade

USER FUNCTION

ATF

Code
////////////////

{User Function: ATF = ADX-Type Filter

                                ...by Bill Blau }

{FORMAT: ATF(Price,r,s) }

Inputs: Price(NumericSeries), r(NumericSimple), s(NumericSimple) ;

ATF = XAverage(AbsValue(XAverage(Price,r)),s) ;

{where Price is a bipolar momentum such as:
    C - C[1]   from the TSI numerator
    HMU - LMD   from the DTI numerator
    Upticks - Downticks from TVI
    C - 0.5*(Highest(H,2)+Lowest(L,2)) from the SMI }

{ Price may also be a bipolar single-smoothed momentum indicator such as
TSI(Price,r,1,1) which replaces XAverage(Price,r) in the above ATF formulation.}

Figure B–24   *ATF: ADX*-Type Filter

USER FUNCTION

SD_TSI

Code
///////////

{User Function: SD_TSI = Slope Divergence TSI Filter

...by Bill Blau }

{FORMAT: SD_TSI(Price,r,s,u,x,y) }

Inputs: Price(NumericSeries), r(NumericSimple), s(NumericSimple),

u(NumericSimple), x(NumericSimple), y(NumericSimple) ;

```
Value1 = TSI(Price,r,s,u) ;
Value2 = DXAverage(Price,x,y) ;

If Value1 - Value1[1] > 0 AND Value2 - Value2[1] > 0 then
      Value3 = Value1
Else
      Value3 = 0 ;

If Value1 - Value1[1] < 0 AND Value2 - Value2[1] < 0 then
      Value4 = Value1
Else
      Value4 = 0 ;

SD_TSI = Value3 + Value4 ;
```

Figure B–25   *SD_TSI:* Slope Divergence *TSI* Filter

REFERENCES

Appel, Gerald (1985). *The Moving Average Convergence-Divergence Trading Method,* Advanced Version, Scientific Investment Systems.

Blau, William (1991). "Double-Smoothed Stochastics," *Technical Analysis of Stocks and Commodities,* Vol. 9, January.

Blau, William (1991). "Double-Smoothed Momenta," *Technical Analysis of Stocks and Commodities,* Vol. 9, May.

Blau, William (1991). "True Strength Index," *Technical Analysis of Stocks and Commodities,* Vol. 9, November.

Blau, William (1991). "True Strength Index & Double-smoothed Stochastics," presented at CompuTrac TAG 14 Technical Analysis Seminar, New Orleans, November 20–22.

Blau, William (1992). "Trading with the True Strength Index," *Technical Analysis of Stocks and Commodities,* Vol. 10, May.

Blau, William (1993). "Stochastic Momentum," *Technical Analysis of Stocks and Commodities,* Vol. 11, January.

Chande, Tushar (1991). "The Midpoint Oscillator," *Technical Analysis of Stocks and Commodities,* Vol. 9, November.

Hutson, Jack K. (1983). "Triple Exponential Smoothing Oscillator: Good TRIX," *Technical Analysis of Stocks and Commodities,* Vol. 1, July/August.

138 • REFERENCES

Lane, George C. (1984). "Lane's Stochastics," *Technical Analysis of Stocks and Commodities,* Vol. 2, March.

Le Beau, Charles, & Lucas, David W. (1992). *Computer Anaysis of the Futures Market,* Business One/Irwin. Homewood, Illinois.

Omega Research, Inc. (1994). *TradeStation™ 3.0* and *SuperCharts™ 2.0* Computer Programs, 9200 Sunset Drive, Miami, Florida 33173, 800-556-2022.

Wilder, J. Welles (1978). *New Concepts in Technical Trading Systems,* Trend Research.

INDEX

and correlation, 11
large interval, 14
and momentum, 13
and noise, 12
and rally, 12–13
Moving average convergence
divergence (*MACD*), 1,
49
MTM, 6

N

Noise, 8–10
Nonambiguous trending and
*DTI*_Trade filter, 67

O

Omega continuous graph, 66
Omega SuperCharts, 2
Code, 109
Omega TradeStation, 2
Code, 109
One-day stochastics, 42
Overbought, 5
Oversold, 5

P

Price direction, 76

R

Relative Strength Index (*RSI*),
1

S

Signal Line and *TSI,* 4
Slope, 7

Slope divergence, 50, 97
and flat prices, 98
and momentum moving
average, 98
and price divergence, 102
and price moving average,
98
and *TSI*_Trade filter, 101
Slope divergence *TSI* filter
(*SD_TSI*), 98
SMI_Trade modes, 85
SMI ADX-Type filter
(*SMI_ATF*), 94
S&P 500, 4
and *SMI,* 31
and virtual close, 61
Stochastics:
*DS*_stochastic, 27–28
fast, 25
slow, 1, 18, 26, 35, 36
stochastic momentum, 28
Stochastic Momentum Index
(*SMI*) and directional
movement, 83
and double smoothing, 30
and large interval, 32
SMI formula, 29
and *SMI*_Trade filter, 84–85
and stochastic momentum,
28
and two-day stochastics, 37

T

T-bonds, 38, 39, 49
Tick volume, 43
Tick Volume Indicator (*TVI*), 1,
43, 44
Ergodic_*TVI* oscillator, 45
and gaps, 43–45

Tick Volume Indicator
  (Continued)
  as intraday indicator, 43
  upticks and downticks, 43
Trading range, congestion, flat
  prices, 1
Trading System:
  and *DTI,* 69
  noise, 69
  and slope divergence,
    100–101
  and *TSI*_Trade, 82
  and *TVI*_Trade, 89
Trend, 3
  and momentum, 17
  and negative slopes, 75
  nonambiguous trends, 17
  and positive slopes, 75
  and *SMI,* 37

True Strength Index (*TSI*),
  1, 3
  TSI formula, 5
  and *TSI*_Trade filter, 81
TSI ADX-Type filter
  (*TSI_ATF*), 93
*TVI*_Trade filter, 87
Two-day stochastic oscillator,
  39–41

V

Virtual close, 61, 68

W

Wilder, J. Welles, Jr., 1, 91, 105